JUNK to Jewelry

A step-by-step guide to using found objects in jewelry you can actually wear

Brenda Schweder

© 2007 Brenda Schweder. All rights reserved. This book may not be reproduced in part or in whole without written permission of the publisher, except in the case of brief quotations used in reviews. Published by Kalmbach Publishing Co., 21027 Crossroads Circle, Waukesha, WI 53186. Distributed to the trade press by Watson-Guptill.

Printed in the United States of America

11 10 09 08 07   1 2 3 4 5

Visit our Web site at kalmbachbooks.com
Secure online ordering available

Publisher's Cataloging-In-Publication Data
(Prepared by The Donohue Group, Inc.)

Schweder, Brenda.
   Junk to jewelry : a step-by-step guide to using found objects in jewelry you can actually wear / Brenda Schweder.

   p. : ill. ; cm.

   Includes bibliographical references.
   ISBN: 978-0-87116-248-9

1. Jewelry making. 2. Found objects (Art) I. Title.

TT212 .S34 2007
739.27

Dremel® is a registered brand name and is used as an adjective to describe the products made by the Dremel® brand.
Slinky® is a registered trademark and is used without permission.

Author's Note
Welcome to the Life of the Found and Altered

My brother-in-law coined the phrase that is one with who I am to my husband's family, "There's a fine line between art and junk!" I'm afraid he was only half joking, but the comment came after a full day of moving our household from one side of the city to another. Somehow he didn't see the necessity of moving boxes and boxes of buttons, old game pieces, paint-by-number sets, and a plethora of other bits and parts. And he was the patient one!

It takes a little grit, a lot of stubbornness, and a smidge of wacky to stand up to the teasing and raised eyebrows that accompany being what I call a *Junque* (my Franglais for "beautiful refuse") Artist. Not to mention you can't be embarrassed to stoop and pick up a treasure on the sidewalk or stop and load an old table left on the side of the road. Your humility takes a back seat to this art form. And really, most master artists are known for their eccentricities, right?

My house is smattered with road-kill furniture, repurposed storm doors, and basic Rummage-o-Rama, so it's not unheard of for my husband to voice time after time, "That's not coming in the house, is it?" regarding a new-to-me dresser or rusty old lawn chair being unloaded from the back of the car. My repeated response sounds something like, "But, these things have history! Just look at this character – patina like this is priceless."

We're told to do what brings us joy, and I believe in using God's gifts of talent to us — so why not recycle when creating?

That's probably the crux of it for us pickers, isn't it? Seeing the beauty in something so ordinary, so overlooked by the crows of the world who say only the new and shiny is valuable. My heart skips a beat when I see an old painted bit of metal on the sidewalk, a cracked piece of back-up-light reflector on the ground next to the gas pump, or an acorn (last year yielded a bumper crop here in Wisconsin). My brain surges with challenge – how can I turn this lovely bit of beauty into something resurrected, something many others can appreciate?

Beauty is all around us, and I mean that in an even larger sense than the splendor of oak trees, mountain ranges, and big, blue skies. That's all fabulous, but the sense of discovery unearthed from the ordinary, via traces of human travel and from within modern archaeological digs, is so enamoring that I feel more than compelled to share them with you.

Brenda Schweder

Table of Contents

Not Lost But Found

What to find, and where to find it

We've all seen the cartoons where a menacing foe envisions his would-be victim as a finished meal, steaming on a plate. The world of found and altered objects evokes similar imagery when one happens upon old and new everyday objects, the stuff of life. Common (and sometimes not so common) items we use, decorate with, and live with seem to reappear. We discover them by seeing them in a different light as they lie on tables in our homes and in stooping to unearth them while we walk, lounge, or pump gasoline. We connect again, doing our daily living.

Items that others see at face value resurface as focal pieces, pendants, clasps, or charms. They are conjured as neck pieces laden with beads or chain, cuffs that wind around wrists, rings that perch atop fingers, earrings that command.

There's a certain intrigue that innovation and reinvention bring. Often when found objects are juxtaposed with other objects the pairing tells a different story. The result is whimsical, clever, and certainly thought-provoking. We can feel virtuous about recycling. We're doing our part for the environment (and this ain't grayed newsprint, baby)!

Literally, anything and everything that appeals to one's sense of wonder – and, in the jewelry realm, can fit in the palm of your hand – is fodder for your next ornamental creation. These treasures, foundlings if you will, hold immediate sentimental value. They gain significance by being singled out or coupled with other special bijoux as wearable embellishments. So, if whatever it is – an old penny, a frayed shoelace, a painted bolt – speaks to you and tugs at your heart, go ahead! Incorporate it into a special adornment.

"Where do you find this stuff?"
One could amass a small fortune for every time an admirer has asked this very question about items in found-object artworks. Just like the eclectic interior design trend, the secret is in cultivating a feeling that such items have been gathered over time. There's no substitute for just that – a lifetime collection from the world-as-treasure-trove – a diary of sorts telling where you've been and when.

The following is a list of way-cool places to lurk about. Remember to take your time and let ideas ripen or mature in your mind as items call to you. Enjoy the journey of collection as much as the making and wearing.

Old-stuff places
These are the obvious choices for choice finds: garage, rummage, or tag sales; estate sales; antique stores; architectural salvage warehouses; auctions; attics; and the homes of lovely sage relatives and friends. Be on the lookout for little tchotchkes, boxes of hardware, jars of buttons, bins of parts, and general tiny treasures. Arrive early or late; these things tend to be overlooked by collectors of whatever's trendy, so your find will be waiting for you.

The weird and the wonderful
Super surplus stores and old storage and warehouse facilities yield finds like test tubes, specimen tins, optical lenses, and jewelry and watch parts, not to mention glove forms, teaching supplies, and an assortment of danger tape. Used book stores yield kitschy housekeeping and scouting manuals, old romance novels, outdated textbooks, and resource books such as picture dictionaries. (Just watch out for the rare book shelves, where prices rise substantially.)

The path to everywhere
Simply look down when you are walking (with dog or not) or if you've stopped to chat. I found a beat-up, palm-sized doll on the curb in downtown Chicago, way-cool metal plugs discarded in back of a tool and die shop in Cherry Valley, Illinois, a fabulous split rock while I was locked out of my car in Tombstone, South Dakota, and the best corally-pink rusty metal shard ever along the beach in Ft. Myers, Florida.

Build it and they will come
Once people see that you enjoy working with what my kids have come to know as "good garbage," it comes to you. Friends, family, and acquaintances come bearing shoe boxes, zip-top bags, and envelopes of goodies they couldn't bear to throw out (we pack rats have weak knees when it comes to garbage day) or just thought you could work some magic with. A friend and local PBS auction volunteer brought me a worn box of dusty and grimy buttons an elderly friend had given him. A sweet and special bit of reciprocity, he left with my collage donation and I got new components for gluing.

Urban digs
Construction sites offer a whole other world of options. A little dirt scuffling, leading a metal detector, or being in the right place at the right (remodeling) time can unearth little bits-cum-baubles at hard-hat sites, after the winter thaw, or even under soon-to-be-replaced floorboards. My youngest brother pressed a handful of old skeleton keys into my palm one day – a gift that is worth a thousand birthdays. He found them in the walls of the bungalow he was helping my sister remodel and thought of me. Brotherly love!

Know a guy who knows a guy
. . . or someone who knows this gal. A former teaching peer happens to be the curator of my alma mater's historic costume collection; I received bits of broken jewelry, lace segments, and a few awesome hand-painted children's hangers. Get to know pawn-shop guys, contractors, and my favorites – owners of salvage places – like my new friends, Leonard and Joe, down on Kinnickinnic Ave. in Milwaukee.

Everyday travels
Along with old goodies you cull from daily jaunts here and there, you can find wonders everywhere you go. The office supply store, hardware store, grocery store, and craft store all harbor trinkets and treasures that when thought about just a little differently, engage and excite. Think about new ways to use new stuff, too. Think out of the cardboard box and into the jewelry box.

All in all, finding good garbage is simply about keeping an eye out for it. If you love cool stuff and neat old things, you'll become a natural at finding found objects.

A final thought ...
The most exciting aspect of finding and altering objects is that you can't just go to the store and buy something, and you won't end up with the same stuff everyone else has. Your art will have a story – your story – whether it's a cherished bit that came from your grandmother, or a special memory of the trip where you found the feather that you added to that certain necklace. I've given you supply lists and instructions to work from and sources where I can, but you won't be able to duplicate these projects exactly. Use this book as your inspiration; make these projects your own by using your things. Most of all, enjoy the journey *and* the scenery along the way.

Tools

sandpaper and emery boards

bench block and hammer

multi-hole punch

letter and number punches

jewelry cleaning cloth

mandrel

Dremel drill and bits

Jewelry-making

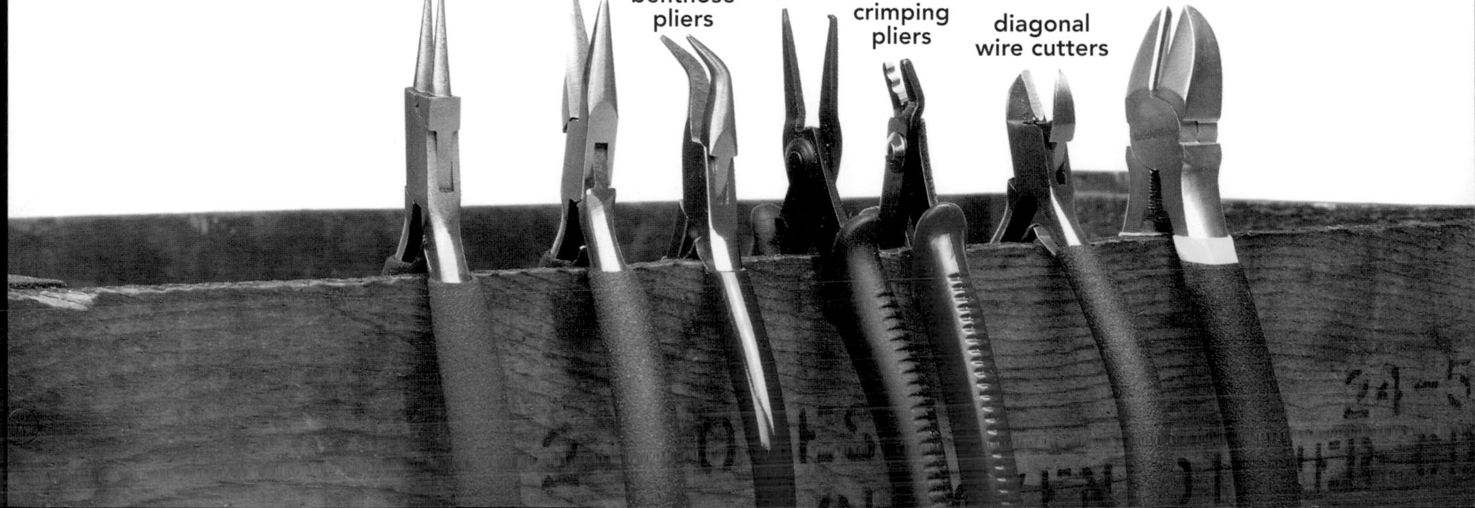

roundnose pliers

chainnose pliers

bentnose pliers

split-ring pliers

crimping pliers

diagonal wire cutters

toolbox or heavy-duty wire cutters

seam
sealant

gel medium

fabric
glue

tacky
glue

Gluing and finishing

E-6000

Bond
527

G-S Hypo
Cement

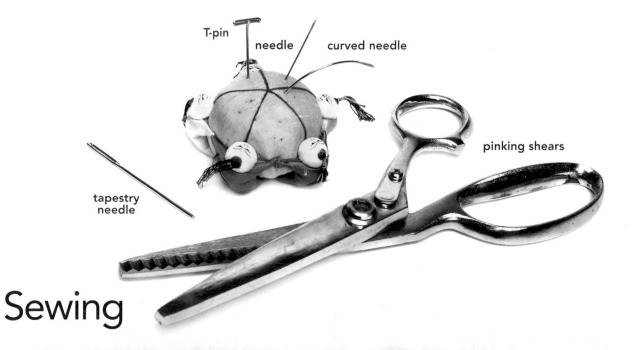

T-pin

needle

curved needle

pinking shears

tapestry
needle

Sewing

Materials

foil tape

bone folder

Paper arts

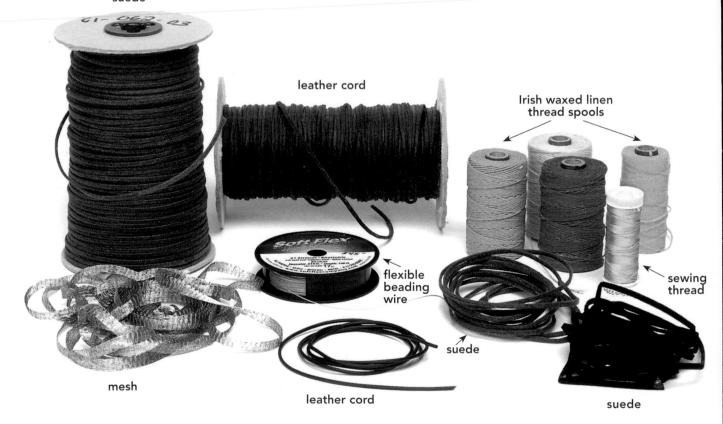

suede

leather cord

Irish waxed linen
thread spools

Soft Flex

flexible
beading
wire

sewing
thread

suede

mesh

leather cord

suede

Knotting and coiling

Jewelry findings

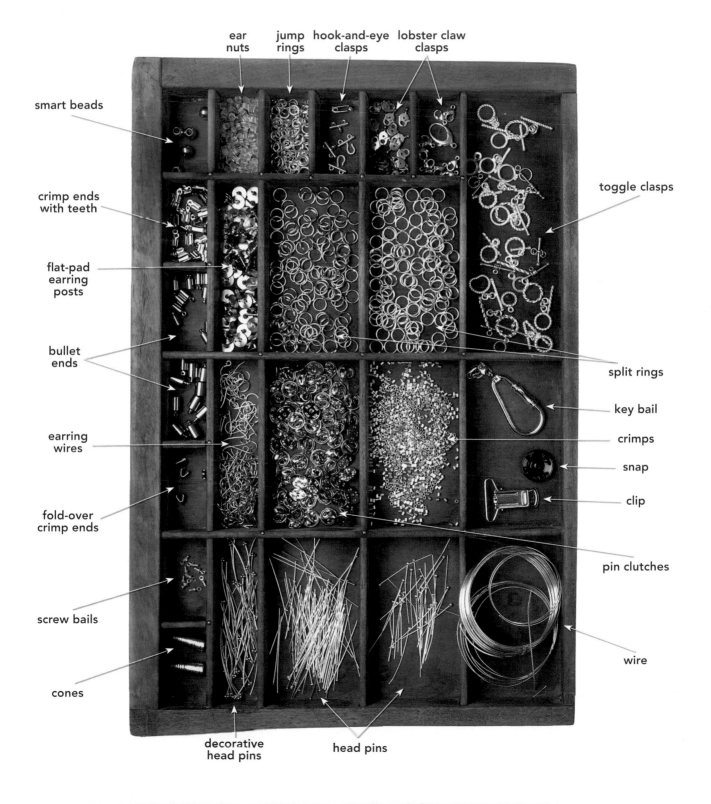

ear nuts

jump rings

hook-and-eye clasps

lobster claw clasps

smart beads

crimp ends with teeth

flat-pad earring posts

bullet ends

earring wires

fold-over crimp ends

screw bails

cones

toggle clasps

split rings

key bail

crimps

snap

clip

pin clutches

wire

decorative head pins

head pins

Techniques

Jewelry-making can be overwhelming until you know your way around a crimp, pliers, or a roll of beading wire. The following techniques are a remedy to newbie-itis and will give you the confidence to make beautiful jewelry in no time at all.

KNOTS

Note: Most knots are secured with an adhesive such as beader's cement, glue, or nail polish. Check project instructions for a suitable choice for each piece.

Lark's head knot

Fold a cord in half and lay it behind a

ring, loop, or bar with the fold pointing down. Bring both ends through the ring from back to front, then through the fold, and tighten.

Overhand knot

1. Make a loop and pass the working end through it.
2. Pull the ends to tighten the knot.

Square knot

1. Cross the left-hand cord over the right-hand cord, and then bring it under the right-hand cord from back to front. Pull it up in front so both ends are facing upward.

2. Cross right over left, forming a loop, and go through the loop again, from back to front. Pull the ends to tighten the knot.

Three-strand braiding

Cut three equal-length strands of cord.

Tie one set of ends in an overhand knot, leaving three long strands. Alternating right and left, bring the outside strand over the center strand. Finish by tying the free ends in an overhand knot.

Slip knot

1. Anchor the tail of the cord in your hand. Make a circle with the working end crossing over the tail. Push the working cord through the back of the circle, making a loop.
2. Pull the loop to tighten the knot. Shorten the loop by pulling on either end of the cord, or lengthen by pulling on the loop.

Surgeon's knot

1. Loop the right end of a cord over the left, as you would to begin to tie your shoe. Loop it around again and pull tight.

2. Cross the left over the right and go through once. Pull tight.

WIRE & METAL TECHNIQUES

Crimp beads are the staples of beading. They're used to attach beading wire to a clasp.

Flattened crimps

1. Hold the crimp using the tip of your chainnose pliers. Tightly squeeze the crimp shut.
2. Check that the crimp has a solid grip on the wire. If the wire slides, remove the old crimp and repeat with a new one.

Jump rings are the paper clips of beading. They connect one part to another; correct the direction a part faces; give energy and movement to your work; or act as one end of a clasp.

Loops and jump rings: opening and closing

1. To open a jump ring or loop, grip both sides of a single ring with two pairs of pliers. Simultaneously, move one hand away from your body and the other toward you. Do not pull the ring apart sideways, or the wire will weaken and possibly break.

2. To close a jump ring or loop, re-grip both sides. Simultaneously, reverse the movement you made to open the ring until both edges meet.

Loops (plain or wrapped) and eyes are the hangers of beading. They hold jump rings and dangle beads or charms. Wrapped loops add strength, security, and a decorative finish.

Plain loop or eye

1. Gently bend the wire end down to form a right angle. Using diagonal wire cutters (with the flush end of the blades toward the piece), cut the wire leaving approximately ⅜ in. (1cm).
2. With roundnose pliers, grip the end of the wire with the pliers' tips. Holding the piece steady, roll the pliers toward you to make half of the loop.

3. Release, reposition your grip, and roll again to complete the loop.
4. The completed plain loop or eye.

Wrapped loop

1. Grip a head pin above the beads with chainnose pliers, and bend the wire to form a 90-degree angle above the pliers, as shown.
2. Grip the wire at the beginning of the right angle with the tips of roundnose pliers.

3. Bend the wire up and around the pliers, as shown.
4. Reposition the roundnose pliers by gripping the wire with the bottom jaw inside the loop. Complete the loop, wrapping the wire end around to a 90-degree angle once more. Note: If you plan to add this component onto a closed ring or loop, add it now before completing the coil.

5. Grip the entire loop with chainnose pliers, holding it steady with your non-dominant hand. Grip the wire end with a second pair of pliers.
6. Wrap the wire around the shank (the space between the loop and where your jewelry starts), keeping the coils close and tight. Note: The gripped end will become bent and "chewed," and you will need to reposition your chainnose pliers several times.
7. When you have completed several coils (only one is necessary; the rest fill in the gap and decorate), use diagonal wire cutters to snip off excess wire close to the coil.
8. Carefully tuck the cut end close to the coil bottom with chainnose pliers. Note: You may need to hold the loop steady with another small pliers while you do this step.

Wrapped swing

1. Center a top-drilled bead on a length of wire. Bend each wire upward so the wires are parallel to each other.
2. Bend and cross the wires into an "X" above the bead.

3. Using chainnose pliers, make a small bend in each wire so the ends form a 90-degree angle.
4. Grip the triangular loop above the bead, and wrap the horizontal wire around the vertical wire as in a wrapped loop. Trim the excess horizontal wire close to the coil. Use the vertical wire to make a plain or wrapped loop, if desired.

Triangular swing

1. Center a top-drilled bead on a length of wire. Bend each wire upward so the wires are parallel to each other.
2. Bend and cross the wires into an "X" above the bead.

3. Using chainnose pliers, make a small bend in the long wire to form a 90-degree angle. Cut the excess short wire where it meets the long wire.

(Not at All) Hard (to) Wear

Spring clip charm-holder necklace

High-end jewelry designers have nothing on this toggle clip charm holder. Charms collected over time deserve a display that befits their significance. This Green Girl Studios pewter heart collection is enhanced with aluminum, nickel, and velvety suede — shiny sterling would just mess things up!

Materials

- **6** 15-25mm pewter beads (Green Girl Studios), or any charm collection
- **3** 4-6mm faceted glass beads
- 58 x 30mm spring hook
- 2 yd. (1.8m) ⅛-in. (3mm) suede or Ultrasuede trim
- 6-12 in. (15-30cm) 4mm chain, gunmetal
- 6-12 in. 2mm chain, silver
- **3** 1½-in. (3.8cm) head pins, gunmetal
- **8** 10mm jump rings, silver
- 6mm jump ring, gunmetal
- **8** 4mm jump rings, silver
- **4** 4mm jump rings, gunmetal
- **2** crimp ends with teeth, gunmetal
- 5 x 12mm lobster claw clasp, gunmetal

Tools

- roundnose pliers
- chainnose pliers
- diagonal wire cutters
- G-S Hypo Cement (optional)

1 Create charms: a) Load a faceted black glass bead on a head pin and turn a plain loop (see Techniques); add the loop to a single 4mm chain link and a 10mm jump ring (Techniques); b) repeat part **a** with another black bead, but add the loop to a 4mm chain segment and a 10mm jump ring; c) open a 4mm gunmetal jump ring, add the loop of a pine cone charm and a 1¼-in. (3.2cm) segment of 4mm chain, close the jump ring, then attach the end link of the chain to a 10mm jump ring; d) load a black bead on a head pin, make a plain loop, add it to the bottom hole of a "love" pendant, attach the top hole to a 2-in. (5cm) segment of 4mm chain with a 4mm gunmetal jump ring, then attach the component to a 10mm jump ring.

2 Create charms: a) (not pictured) Attach a 4mm silver jump ring to one end of a 1¼-in. (3.2cm) length of 2mm chain, add the "key" heart bead, then open and close a 4mm silver jump ring around the remaining end link and a 10mm jump ring; b) repeat with a 1-in. (2.5cm) length of 2mm chain and the "armor" heart; c) repeat with a 2-in. length of 2mm chain and the "laced" heart; d) string the "sacred" heart onto a 2¼-in. (5.7cm) length of chain, open a 4mm silver jump ring, add both end links of the chain and a 10mm jump ring, and close the 4mm jump ring.

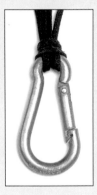

3 Cut two lengths of suede trim to 2 in. longer than your desired length (mine are 32 in./ 81cm). Center and make a lark's head knot (Techniques) around the top of the spring hook.

4 Open a 4mm gunmetal jump ring and attach to the end of a crimp end loop and a 6mm jump ring; close the jump ring. Connect both raw ends of suede trim to the crimp ends by inserting and pinching tightly with chainnose pliers. (Add a drop of G-S Hypo Cement for extra security.) Attach the lobster claw clasp to the other side with a 4mm gunmetal jump ring. Open the spring hook and add the charm components as desired.

Designer's Tip

Don't be afraid to institute your creative license when the design calls for it. Sideways hearts are definitely a little left-of-center, but work in this particular instance.

Alternative

- Substitute your own collection of art beads and/or other charms for the pewter beads.
- Substitute another type of toggle clip or another metal type, and theme accordingly.

Biker Chic(k)

Bicycle chain necklace

Rules of the road. 1) Do NOT disassemble your bicycle to try this project at home. 2) A little degreaser goes a long, long way. 3) Isn't it funny how crystal goes with everything? Where edge meets bling, this necklace goes with cashmere or tattoos.

1 Choose the crystals to add to the bicycle chain. Add bicone crystals by loading the crystal on an eye pin and inserting the pin through what will be the bottom of the necklace. Then load a black 6º seed bead. Adjust to size (include ⅜ in./1cm to form the loop), trim, and make a plain loop (see Techniques). For top-drilled crystals, use wire or trim the loops from the eye pins. Then, load the crystal, create a swing (Techniques), insert the chain, and load a 6º seed bead. Adjust the size, trim, and make a plain loop at the end. Begin in the center of the chain and add crystals to both sides.

2 Determine the finished length of your necklace. Subtract the length of the bicycle chain and the clasp. Cut the mesh tubing to twice this length plus ½ in. (1.3cm). Thread the tubing through the end link of the chain and center. Pinch a fold-over crimp end around both pieces just above the link, to secure (clip off the loop extension and file, if necessary).

3 Trim any excess mesh from the remaining strand ends, thread the mesh through the jump ring on the lobster claw clasp (leaving a ½-in. tail), and secure with another fold-over crimp end. Link the lobster claw clasp to the end of the bicycle chain.

Materials
- 14-in. (36cm) bicycle chain
- **18-20** bicone 5301 and pendant Swarovski crystals, in assorted sizes and colors (black diamond, jet, crystal silver shade, crystal, crystal AB, white alabaster, white opal)
- **18-20** 6º seed beads, black
- 30-in. (76cm) 7.5mm width hollow mesh tubing (Rings & Things)
- **18-20** 1½-in. (3.8cm) eye pins, gunmetal (Rings & Things) or **14-16** eye pins and 6 in. (15cm) 22-gauge wire
- **2** fold-over crimp ends
- 20mm lobster claw clasp with small jump ring

Tools
- chainnose pliers
- roundnose pliers
- diagonal wire cutters
- scissors
- emery board or other small file

DESIGNER'S TIP
For uniformly sized plain loops, mark your roundnose pliers with a marker at the tip; working at this same spot guarantees your loops will be the same size.

ALTERNATIVE
- Substitute other hardware bits for the crystals.
- Substitute chain for the mesh tubing.

Ring, Ring, 'RRRRings

Recycled earrings and rings charm bracelet

Here's when being the recipient of your buddy's jewelry box purge gets golden. You could be gifted with pieces from art show artisans, old charm bracelets, rings with great patina, earrings without mates, and broken-clasped necklaces. What's old is new again. Reduce, recycle, reuse — full circle!

1 Begin with a charm bracelet from your jewelry box or a rummage or tag sale, flea market, or second-hand store.

2 Arrange a selection of rings around the bracelet. Open a jump ring, add a link and a ring, and close the jump ring (see Techniques). Repeat with the remaining rings.

3 Repeat step 2, substituting earrings (with earring wires removed) and earring parts for the rings.

4 Repeat step 2, substituting more charms for the rings.

5 **Optional Embellishment** • From copper or brass sheeting, cut small, unstructured shapes with a tin snips or jewelry saw. Stamp with letter or number punches, and sand edges.

6 Create a hole with a multi-hole punch (or drill) and add patina by immersing the charms in liver of sulfur according to the manufacturer's directions. Repeat step 2 to attach the stamped charms to the bracelet.

Materials
- charm bracelet
- variety of rings, earring pieces, charms, pendants
- various sizes of jump rings
- sheeting, .005 to .008 thickness, copper or brass (hardware stores) (optional)

Tools
- 2 pairs of pliers

Optional tools:
- number and letter punches
- multi-hole punch or other hole punch or drill
- hammer
- sandpaper
- tin snips or jewelry saw
- liver of sulfur

Loop-de-Hoops

Recycled chain necklace
hoop earrings

A jewelry box is like a time capsule. It holds your favorites from today, but languishing in the back are the gems from your past. It's time to reclaim those giant '80s hoops! While you're at it, grab any broken or knotted chains. With a simple twist and twirl, you've made the modern connection and you've got a new favorite pair.

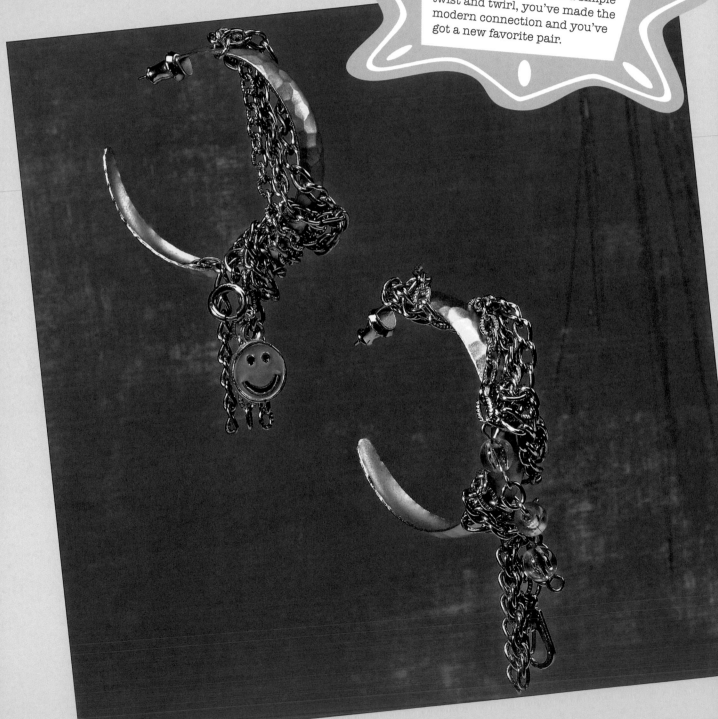

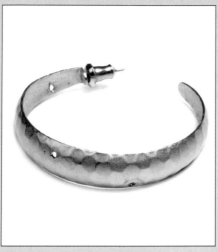

Materials
- pair of gold hoop earrings
- 10-12 in. (25-30cm) each of **2-4** chain types in silver and gold
- **4-10** charms, extra clasps, or brand tags
- **6** 6mm jump rings
- **4-10** 3-4mm jump rings

Tools
- **2** pairs of pliers
- diagonal wire cutters
- Dremel or other hand-held drill with ¹⁄₁₆-in. (2mm) bit
- jewelry cleaning cloth

1 Polish the hoop earrings and the chain with a cleaning cloth. Cut the selections of chain into 5- or 6-in. (13-15cm) lengths, two lengths of each kind of chain. (Note: Vary the lengths a bit to create interest at the bottom.) Put one set of chain lengths aside.

2 Mark and drill three holes on a hoop earring, alternating sides, one near the top, one at the front, and one near the back.

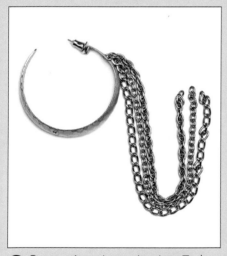

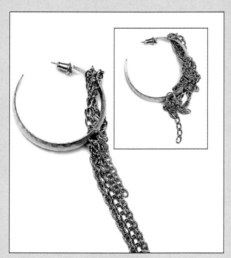

3 Open a 6mm jump ring (see Techniques) and pick up the end links of three longer chain lengths and the top drill hole. Close the jump ring.

DESIGNER'S TIP

Before drilling, tap the marks with a hammer and awl to prevent the drill bit from skating off-mark.

4 Wrap the chain around the earring and use a 6mm jump ring to secure it to the second drill hole, adding a shorter piece of a different chain type. Continue wrapping chain and secure with a third jump ring to the final drill hole, allowing tails of chain to dangle.

5 Use 3-4mm jump rings to add clasps, charms, brand tags and/or other beads to the end fringes. Make a second earring to match the first, using the lengths of chain set aside in step 1.

ALTERNATIVE
Drill holes down the center of a pair of hoops and attach in a linear fashion without wrapping the chain.

The Stroke of Midnight

Cinderella watch ribbon bracelet

Mementos come in many shapes and colors, and this one's definitely in-the-pink. A trip to the jeweler revealed the childhood prize as-was couldn't be repaired. But, just as Cinderella's little friends turned rags to riches, this watch turned from timepiece to showpiece by trapping a few tiny charms and sparkles beneath its crystal for some kinetic fun.

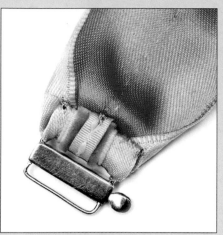

1 Cut ribbon lengths to 10 in. (25cm), and layer the two narrower pieces to the center of the satin piece. Add the watch face to the center of the ribbons by gently prying out the watchband pins (I used my diagonal wire cutters to get at the tiny spring-loaded pins), gathering the ribbon in and replacing the pins. Open a 4mm jump ring (see Techniques), attach the crown charm, and close the jump ring. Link the charm to the watch stem with an 8mm jump ring.

2 Prepare the remaining charms by: a) attaching a 4mm jump ring or b) creating a wrapped swing (Techniques).

3 Arrange the charms for each side. Working from the watch outward, add the loop of a single charm to the blue ribbon and sew in place. (Note: Tack the ribbon in place by piercing all three layers, but anchor the knot and move to the next charm between the satin and velveteen ribbons.) Continue until all the charms for one side are added, then tack the remaining ribbon together in ¼-in. (6mm) increments.

4 Check the fit of the bracelet. Trim with pinking shears to fit your wrist measurement, leaving 1 in. (2.5cm) extra on each side. Apply Dritz Fray Check to the edges and let dry. Fold in the corners of the trim and add a clasp half. Fold the pinked edge under and tack down at the center, then again against the folded ribbon. (This will prevent unsightly needle marks in the satin). Repeat on the other side.

5 Remove the crystal from the watch face and add small crystals and charms inside. Replace the crystal.

Designer's Tip
• Ask your local watch-repair shop to lift the crystal of your favorite no-longer-running watch, then add a few miniature trinkets of your own and replace the crystal.
• If you would like to repair and use your broken watch, watchmakers may be able to retrofit a new movement in the existing casing. You may have to sacrifice the arms (and the value will decrease without the original workings), but you will be able to use an old favorite once more!

Alternative
Attach a pinch clasp at each end, and attach a lobster claw clasp to one end and a jump ring to the other.

Materials
- Cinderella or other novelty watch
- themed charms: kettle, needle and thread, scissors, mouse, crown, high-heel slippers
- 14-16mm faceted glass heart
- 14mm vintage Swarovski faceted heart pendant, comet ore
- 12mm pumpkin bead, ceramic
- **3-5** 3mm bicone 5301 crystals
- **2-3** bird charms (Fire Mountain Gems)
- 1 ft. (30cm) pink satin ribbon, reversible to fuchsia
- 1 ft. pink velveteen ribbon, ½-in. (1.3cm) wide
- 1 ft. baby blue decorative ribbon, ³⁄₁₆-in. (5mm) wide
- baby blue sewing thread
- 1 ft. 22-gauge sterling silver or German jewelry wire
- **3-8** 4mm jump rings, silver
- **8mm** jump ring, silver
- slide clasp (Jess Imports)
- Dritz Fray Check

Tools
- chainnose pliers
- roundnose pliers
- diagonal wire cutters
- pinking shears
- scissors
- sewing needle

A Good Clip

Paper clip necklace-and-earring set

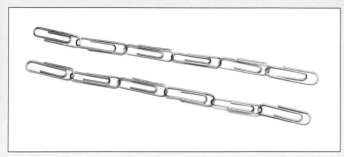

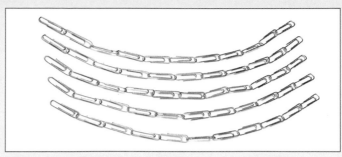

1 necklace • Connect six paper clips from longer curve to shorter curve. Make two sets.

2 Connect 11 paper clips from longer curve to shorter curve. Make five sets.

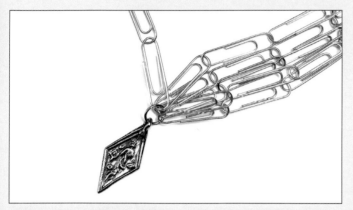

3 Open a 6mm jump ring (see Techniques), load the end clips of one end of all five 11-clip sets, one end of one 6-clip set and one bronze ethnographic charm. Close the jump ring. Repeat on the other side.

4 Open a jump ring, load the remaining end of the clip component and the loop from one half of the toggle clasp, and close the jump ring. Repeat on the other side with the other clasp half.

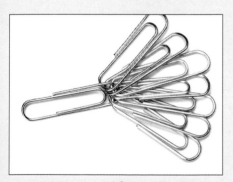

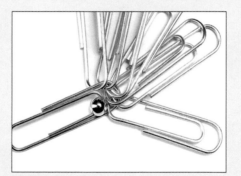

1 earrings • Load five paper clips to the shorter curve of another clip.

2 Load a round bead to the longer curve of the same clip.

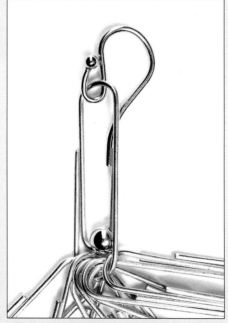

3 Open the earring wire and attach it to the top curve. Repeat steps 1-3 to make a second earring.

Materials
necklace
- box of 100 standard 1-in. (2.5cm) paper clips, gold-tone
- **2** 30-35mm charms, bronze (Ashes to Beauty Adornments)
- **4** 6mm jump rings, gold-filled
- 8mm toggle clasp, gold-tone

earrings
- **16** standard 1-in. paper clips
- **2** 4mm round beads, gold
- pair of earring wires, gold-filled

Tools
- **2** pairs of pliers

Band-waggin'

Rubber band neck ring
and earrings

Sometimes a design just puts itself together. Simple elements juxtapose when matte, primary-colored rubber bands and black rubber washers pair with shiny sterling; bouncy meets hardened. Still, curves are curves and minimal wins — this round.

1 necklace • Begin in the center of the necklace ring with a blue rubber band. Make a lark's head knot (see Techniques) by placing the rubber band under the neck ring and pulling the bottom loop up and through the top. Pull the bottom loop through and down making sure the band lies symmetrically.

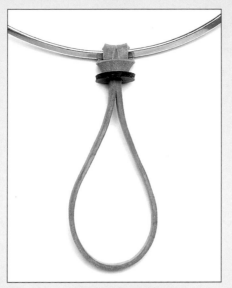

2 Set the knot in place by threading the bottom loop of the rubber band with a rubber washer and pushing it up, just under the knot.

3 Repeat steps 1 and 2 to add the rest of the rubber bands (yellow, red, green, blue) and washers, working outward in both directions.

1 earrings • Repeat steps 1 and 2 of the necklace to make an earring unit, substituting a 10mm soldered jump ring for the necklace ring.

2 Open an earring wire and connect the jump ring. Close the earring wire. Make a second earring to match the first.

Materials
necklace
- **21 ⅛-in. (3mm) rubber bands; 6 red, 5 blue, 6 yellow, 4 green** (office supply store)
- **21 size ⁵⁄₃₂-in. inner-dimension x ⅜-in. outer-dimension (4mm x 10mm) washers, matte black** (hardware store)
- neck ring, silver (Rio Grande)

earrings
- **2 rubber bands, same color**
- **2 ⁵⁄₃₂-in. inner-dimension x ⅜-in. outer-dimension washers, matte black**
- **2 10mm soldered jump rings**
- pair of earring wires

Tools
2 pairs of pliers

Stay Connected

Colorful data wire necklace

1 Group and twist together all the shorter data wire strands. Insert the wires through the aquatic tubing and cut wire ends flush to the tube ends.

Materials
- **5-6** 20 in. (51cm) strands data wire, various colors
- 36 in. (.9m) strand data wire, in accent color
- 16½ in. (41.9cm) 4mm inner-dimension standard aquatic air line tubing (pet store, fish department)
- **3** 4mm jump rings
- **6 x 9mm** bullet ends with loop, silver (Rings & Things)
- **10mm** lobster claw clasp, silver
- **3 or 4 in.** (7.6 or 10cm) curb chain, silver

Tools
- **2** pairs of pliers
- scissors or wire cutters
- G-S Hypo Cement

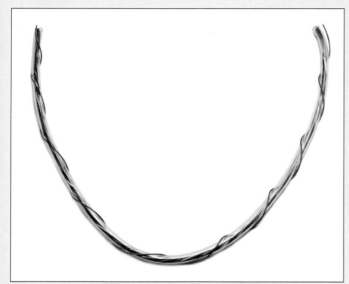

2 Cut 24 in. (61cm) from the longer piece of wire and wind it around the outside of the tubing. Cut the wire flush to the tube ends. Check the fit, and trim wire and tubing if necessary.

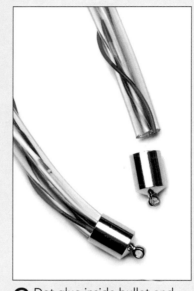

3 Dot glue inside bullet end and slip over tubing and data wire. Repeat on the other side and let dry.

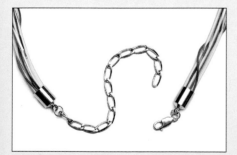

4 Attach the lobster claw clasp to one side of the necklace by opening a jump ring (see Techniques), stringing the clasp ring and the loop on the bullet end, and closing the jump ring. Attach the curb chain length to the other side in the same manner.

5 With the remaining wire piece, form a simple flower charm with a loop.

6 Attach the charm to the end of the chain length with a jump ring.

ALTERNATIVE

- Use all one color wiring for a monochromatic theme.
- Make a large version of the wire charm to add as a pendant.

Alotta' Pull

Drawer pull charm bracelet

FROM URBAN DIGS   38

Isn't it a natural tendency to try on furniture hardware while perusing a flea market or browsing through an antique store? Just don't get caught unscrewing pieces from a vintage Biedermeier. You would need alotta' pull to get out of that tight spot!

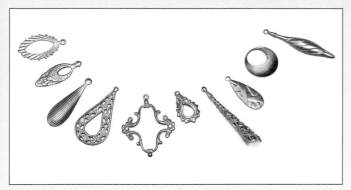

1 Arrange stampings in the order you would like them on the bracelet.

2 Cut the chain long enough to complete a bracelet length figuring in the width of the drawer pull. Space the quantity of stampings to the chain length. Starting from one side, open a 4mm jump ring (see Techniques), load a stamping loop and the bottom of the first chain link, and close the jump ring. Repeat to add all stampings, being careful to keep the stampings facing in the same direction.

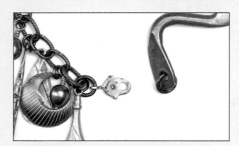

3 Figure the spacing for the pearls. Load a pearl on a head pin and form the first half of a wrapped loop (Techniques) above the beads. String a chain link and complete the wraps. Continue until all of the pearl components are added.

4 Add the chain to the drawer pull by opening a 6mm jump ring, adding an end chain link and the drill hole from one end of the pull, and closing jump ring.

5 Add the clasp by opening a 4mm jump ring, stringing the remaining end chain link and the clasp loop and closing the jump ring. Add a 6mm jump ring to the remaining end of the drawer pull.

Materials
- discarded dresser drawer pull (with drilled ends)
- 5-in. (13cm) chain segment, brass
- **10** vintage stampings, brass (Stone Mountain Colorado)
- **9** 6-8mm pearls
- **9** 2-in. (5cm) head pins, brass (Vintaj)
- **11** 4mm jump rings
- **2** 6mm jump rings
- **8** x 18mm lobster claw clasp, brass (Vintaj)

Tools
- roundnose pliers
- chainnose pliers
- diagonal wire cutters

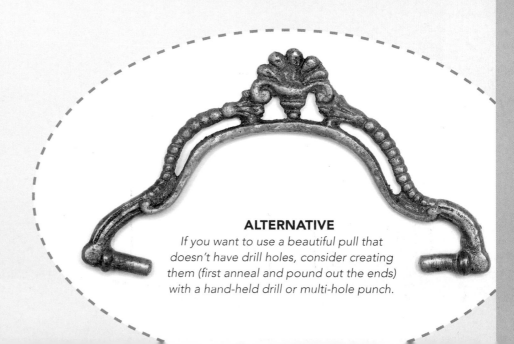

ALTERNATIVE
If you want to use a beautiful pull that doesn't have drill holes, consider creating them (first anneal and pound out the ends) with a hand-held drill or multi-hole punch.

Keyhole
Conundrum

Keys and keyhole escutcheons
purse trick

The key to this easy project is
in the combination of old with
new, bright with patinated.
The trick is to find an appeal-
ing collection of keys and keyhole escutcheons. And, the
conundrum is to figure out
which combination opens
the door to, say, success or
the Nirvana Bead Shop.

1 Open a jump ring (see Techniques). Load the end link of the figure 8 chain and the end link of the key-ring extension. Close the jump ring.

2 Prepare keys or keyhole escutcheons that need special connectors by creating a wrapped swing (Techniques) using a 3-in. (7.6cm) length of wire for each.

Materials
- brass key ring with chain (Rio Grande)
- **9-12** keys
- **9-12** keyhole escutcheons
- 1 yd. (.9m) or more 22-gauge wire, gold-filled or German jewelry wire (longer length may be necessary if used in place of jump rings with escutcheons)
- 4½ in. (11.4cm) matte figure 8 chain, gold-filled
- **18-24** 5mm jump rings, gold filled

Tools
- chainnose pliers
- roundnose pliers
- second pair of chainnose pliers (optional)
- diagonal wire cutters

3 Open a jump ring to connect each key to a link of chain. Close the jump rings.

4 Open a jump ring to connect each escutcheon to a link of chain. Close the jump rings.

designer's tip

Pre-arrange the keys and escutcheons to ensure that different metals and patinas are spaced apart.

Straight Flush on a Sunday Morning

Reversible color-coded
key chain belt

You never know when you will need just the right belt for that Friday night poker game with the girls. This one connects quickly with the ultimate in split ring choices – the key chain size. Reversible to your favorite Sunday comic strips, you can place your bet on a bit of comic relief.

2 Open flaps on key chains, assemble inserts back to back in each key chain, and close flaps.

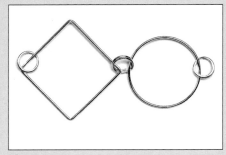

1 Trace and cut selected areas from playing cards and comic strips (eight each), using the cardboard insert from the key chain as a pattern.

3 Assemble connecting components as follows: one split ring, one diamond, one split ring, one circle, one split ring. My belt is 28½ in. (72.4cm) long and uses seven connecting components.

Materials

- assorted comic strip panels
- old or new deck of cards
- color-coded key chain 8-pack (office supply store)
- **31-37** 8mm split rings
- **10-12** 25mm circle components, silver (Silver City)
- **10-12** 25mm diamond/square components, silver (Silver City)
- **3-4** 38mm eye-shaped compo-nents, silver (Silver City)
- **22.5 x 12mm** lobster claw clasp, silver (Rio Grande)

Tools

- scissors
- pencil
- split ring pliers (optional)

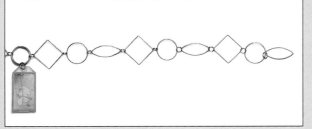

4 Arrange the order of the key chains and add one connecting component between each, being sure to keep the same motif (cards or cartoons) facing up.

5 Create the end component (mine is 13 in./33cm) as follows: split ring, diamond, split ring, circle, split ring, eye shape, and repeat twice more. Attach to one end of the key chain component. Check the fit of the belt, and add or remove elements, as needed.

6 Connect the clasp to the other end of the belt with a split ring.

Designer's Tip:
Be sure the belt components aren't twisted as you attach the key chains from the bottoms of the rings.

Alternative:
Substitute ephemera such as love letters, wallpaper, wrapping paper, newspaper, photos, or any flat, easy-to-cut items for the playing cards and/or cartoons.

Junk ~~Yard~~ Drawer Dawg

Junk drawer miscellany watch

Be brave! The contents of your junk drawer will never find their rightful places in the house, so use them to make a super-duper watch. Cull a variety of items sized no larger than a quarter and lump them together. Then tie it all together with the extra shoelaces you'll never need. When you're done, you might not remember that the orange doodad is the main component to making the vacuum vacuum, but you'll have a great-looking art-to-wear piece instead.

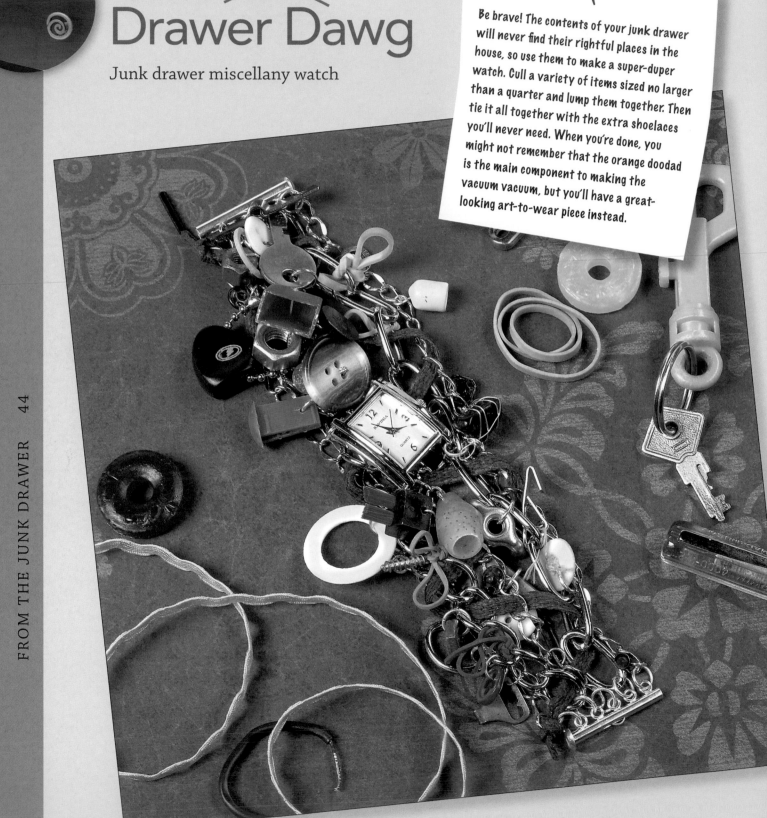

Materials
- watch face with drill holes
- 24 in. (61cm) 7 x 9mm heavy hammered curb chain, silver (Rings & Things)
- 7½ in. (19.1cm) 11 x 21mm jumbo cable oval chain, silver (Rings & Things)
- 7½ in. 11 x 14mm jumbo hammered curb chain, silver (Rings & Things)
- 20-30 junk drawer items
- 30 in. (76cm) waxed shoelace, brown
- 2-5 rubber bands, a variety of sizes
- 1-3 ft. (30-90cm) 22-gauge German jewelry wire, silver
- 20-30 jump rings, a variety of sizes, silver
- 10 6mm jump rings, silver
- 3-5 in. (7.6-13cm) bead chain
- 5-loop slide clasp

Tools
- chainnose pliers
- roundnose pliers
- diagonal wire cutters
- Dremel or other hand-held drill with 1/32-in. bit

1 Create charms by either a) stringing jump rings (see Techniques) sized to the chain; b) creating a wrapped swing (Techniques) (drill if necessary); c) creating a wonky wrap (see p. 73); d) connecting with bead chain; or e) creating a coil loop with plain loop or a plain loop itself (Techniques).

2 Determine the finished length of your bracelet and cut the curb chain into three lengths to equal that measurement, less ½ in. Attach the lengths to the middle and end loops of the 5-loop slide clasp with a 6mm jump ring (Techniques). Attach the other chain types to the second and fourth loops in the same way.

3 Tie the shoelace to the end link at the upper left corner of the bracelet. Then, weave a zigzag pattern, ending by tying it to the bottom left corner. Trim and fray this end.

4 Attach the watch face at an angle with the jump rings.

5 Add large charm components.

6 Add small charm components.

7 Tie on a few rubber bands with surgeon's knots (Techniques).

DESIGNER'S TIP

- Use your hand-held drill to make holes to connect a watch with spring pins.

ALTERNATIVE

- Use themed junk: office junk could mean office supplies and secret-stash candy wrappers; powder-room junk may be assorted toothpaste caps, eye shadow brushes, and bits of cosmetic sponge.

A-Lure-Ring

Adjustable fishing lure rings

Don't wear this ring on your next canoe trip 'cause you may catch an extra boat-partner. While not necessarily the taste of all Ladies-Who-Lunch, your trendy right-hand ring will weigh in with a first prize from your fishing buddies. Way to lure 'em in!

1 **zebra bug ring** • Glue a few seed beads to the sharp ends of the lure's hook with G-S Hypo Cement. Center the wire length around the middle of the lure body, embedding the wire in the pipe cleaner and twisting firmly at the bottom.

2 Add the glass wired flowers to the outer rim of the mesh dome top. On the underside, tightly anchor by creating a plain loop (see Techniques). If there is extra slack on the head pin, make a double loop on one side.

3 Load two or three black glass beads to five or six ball-tipped head pins and add to the mesh dome with a wrapped loop.

4 Add the lure component to the center of the mesh dome top by wiring through two different holes and twisting the wire tightly together close to the underside.

5 Trim the wire ends and tuck close to the top. Add the ring component by fitting on the mesh dome top and folding the ring tabs over it.

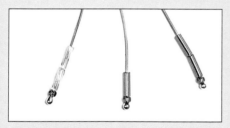

1 **bee ring** • Load a seed bead and one or more green bugle beads on the ball-tipped head pins.

2 Add each to the mesh dome top with a coil wrap leaving the center holes open.

3 The completed back view. Prepare the bee as in step 1 of the zebra bug ring, then repeat steps 4 and 5 to complete the bee ring.

Materials
both projects
• mesh top ring component
• G-S Hypo Cement
bee version
• bee fishing lure (antique store)
• assorted green bugle and 11º seed beads

• **20-24** 1½-in. (3.8cm) ball-tipped head pins, silver
• **4** in. (10cm) 22- or 24-gauge wire
zebra bug version
• zebra bug fishing lure (antique store)
• **4** 15mm vintage yellow wired flowers (Stone Mountain Colorado)
• **10** 4mm black glass or onyx rondelles

• **3** 6º or 8º seed beads
• **6** 1½ in. ball-tipped head pins, silver
• **4** in. (10cm) 22- or 24-gauge wire
Tools
• roundnose pliers
• chainnose pliers
• diagonal wire cutters
• toolbox cutters

Just North of Here

Compass and topographic map ring

Knowing where you are is a plus most of the time. Knowing how to do it with style? That's where this ring comes in. Fashioned out of a pin-type compass and topographic map that's been printed on water-proof mapping paper, you'll never again lose your bearing.

1 Cut the pin from a pin-type compass.

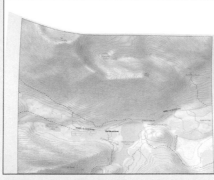

2 On your computer, select a map section with contour lines in concentric circles, 1½ in. (3.8cm) in diameter and smaller.

Materials

- pin-type compass (camping departments of hunting/fishing/hiking stores)
- National Geographic Adventure Paper (http://maps.nationalgeographic.com/topo/adventure.cfm)
- 20-gauge square sterling silver wire, half-hard

Tools

- ring mandrel
- sharp scissors
- toolbox cutters
- sandpaper
- computer and computer printer

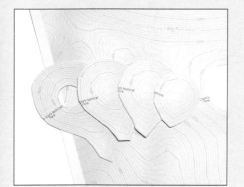

3 Print four identical maps and cut out consecutively larger areas from the contour circle. Place the base of the compass in the middle of the concentric circles and trace. Cut about ⅛ in. (3mm) inside the mark for a snug fit. Repeat with each of the remaining three maps, lining up the markings and tracing the next circles from the middle of the first.

4 Apply the paper pieces to the compass base, smallest to largest, and line them up, again matching the markings.

5 Cut the wire length in half and thread it through the hole that formerly housed the pin. Turn the ring around and use the ring mandrel to size the wire. Form the correct size by wrapping the wire to the center back, twisting and doubling back.

6 Wrap to the top again, and wrap haphazardly sideways to secure. Trim close, and sand ends smooth.

DESIGNER'S TIP

If you are computer-phobic, buy a topographic map at a hunting/fishing/hiking store and prepare it at a copy shop. You may need to ask for help as the Adventure Paper is a bit thicker than normal copy paper.

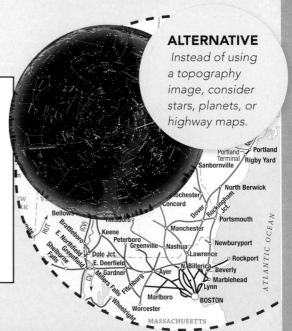

ALTERNATIVE

Instead of using a topography image, consider stars, planets, or highway maps.

49 · JUNK TO JEWELRY

Wound 'n' Wound We Go

Slinky® coil bracelet

House rule: When toys aren't picked up after a day (or ten), they become the property of Mom the Jewelry Designer, like it or not. This Slinky® looks great when adorned with dangles — a bit of whimsy that comes with a bonus: toy-free floors.

Materials
- plastic spring-style toy
- **8-12** vintage Lucite charms or African trade beads
- 20mm or larger vintage Lucite bead or pendant (optional)
- **8-12** 9mm split rings
- **5** or more 6-8mm Smart Beads, silver or gold

Tools
- diagonal wire cutters
- toolbox cutters
- emery board or fine sandpaper
- split-ring pliers (optional)

1 Cut the spring to the desired length (this project uses 7-16 rings). Smooth the rough edges with an emery board or sandpaper.

2 Add split rings to the loops of vintage Lucite charms or African trade beads. (Note: If the beads do not hang freely, use toolbox cutters to trim a bit from the split ring, or use a jump ring.)

3 Add a Smart Bead to one end of the bracelet (the core of the bead will conform to the shape of the plastic piece and stay put). Divide the charms into four groups and add one group to the bracelet, working it down to the end bead. Add another Smart Bead and Lucite charm grouping, alternating until only one Smart Bead remains. Space the Smart Beads as desired around the bracelet rings. Add a Smart Bead to the end.

ALTERNATIVE

- Attach beads instead of charms — just load onto head pins and turn a plain loop (see Techniques).

- Attach charms with jump rings. I used split rings because they mimicked the look of the spring toy, but they can be tough to work with, especially with larger charms.

Personal Party Kit

Balloon drop earrings
and necklace

Want to be celebration-ready wherever you go? Wear this balloon pendant-and-earring set and be the life of the party. Insert simple plastic washers inside small balloons and add a touch of whimsy and color to your special-occasion frock. And, they are super-light, so you won't be weighed down while you paint the town red — or orange, or blue, or green, or . . .

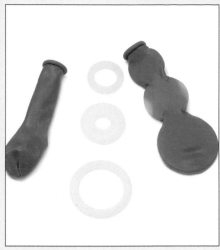

1 earrings • Carefully open the neck of a balloon with your fingers and insert the largest washer into the bottom so that the latex is stretched taut. Repeat with the medium, then the small washer, placing them parallel to the largest washer.

2 Cut four 6-in. (15cm) lengths of linen. Tie a square knot (see Techniques) around the meeting points between washers, ending at the center back. (Note: Play with the tightness to get a pleasing look.) Tie another square knot (Techniques) at the top of the balloon to close it.

3 Tie on the ear stud by passing the linen both ways through the stud loop and making another square knot. Trim close and carefully dot with glue. Add the earring nut. Make a second earring to match the first.

Materials
earrings
- 2 small party balloons (party supply store, grocery store)
- 2 ⅝-in. (1.6cm) outer-dimension plastic washers (hardware store)
- 2 ¾-in. (1.9cm) outer-dimension plastic washers (hardware store)
- 2 1-in. (2.5cm) outer-dimension plastic washers (hardware store)
- pair 13 x 10mm enamel ear studs with loop, (Fire Mountain Gems)
- 2 earring nuts
- 4 ft. (1.2m) Irish waxed linen thread, color to match balloons

necklace
- medium party balloon
- ⅝-in. (1.6cm) outer-dimension plastic washer (hardware store)
- ¾-in. (1.9cm) outer-dimension plastic washer (hardware store)
- 1 in. (2.5cm) outer-dimension plastic washer (hardware store)
- 13 x 10mm enamel charm with loop, (Fire Mountain Gems)
- 4 ft. (1.2m) Irish waxed linen thread, color to match balloons
- wire necklace (Rings & Things)

Tools
- scissors or wire cutters
- G-S Hypo Cement or cyanoacrylate glue

1 necklace • Repeat steps 1-3 of the earrings, substituting an enamel charm for the earring stud and nut in step 3. Thread the pendant onto a wire necklace and tie a surgeon's knot (Techniques). Center the pendant on the necklace wire.

designer's tip
- Play with the washers within the balloon to achieve a playful shape.

Crafty Spanish Dancer

Craft stuff doll necklace

Sugar and spice and everything nice, that's what little girls are made of. Unless you are a Crafty Spanish Dancer Girl – then you are made of various and sundry craft-table items and a magic wave of the Create-O-Wand (two waves gets you red hair). The only things missing? A little merengue music and two tiny maracas. Olé!

1 Make the skirt: Cut 2 ft. (61cm) of fuchsia waxed linen. Bunch the feathers and wrap the linen around the quill end (blue thread used here for illustration). Knot the ends.

2 Make the body: Cut another 2 ft. of fuchsia linen, thread it onto a wide-eyed needle, and pierce through the coil perpendicularly at the center. Tie a square knot (see Techniques) just above it. Then, sew the thread through the wooden flower bead, the Japanese spoke bead, the wooden girl bead, and the center of the crocheted circle.

3 Take up the slack and tie another square knot just above the doll component. Create a ½- to 1-in. (1.3-2.5cm) loop and tie a knot below the last square knot to secure it.

4 Add the arms: Cut the remaining fuchsia linen into three equal lengths. Center and tie a square knot with all three around the doll-component linen just below the spoke bead. Thread one side of the three linen lengths onto a needle and pierce all through a felted wool ball. Remove the needle, snug the ball up to the spoke bead, and braid (Techniques) for ¾ in. (1.9cm). Tie an overhand knot (Techniques), thread a glass bead onto one of the strands, and tie a square knot beneath it. Trim ends to ¼ in. (6mm). Repeat to form the second arm.

Alternative
Paint a face on a wooden bead you find at a craft store or use Mod-Podge to glue on a face cut from a magazine or book.

5 Embellish the chain: Thread the orange linen through the wide-eyed needle and lace back and forth through the large links of the figaro chain, leaving a 3 in. (7.6cm) tail on both ends.

6 On one side, thread back through a few links and tie a square knot. Trim close and dot with glue. Rethread the linen and repeat on the other side to finish. Open a jump ring (Techniques), string an end link from one end of the chain and the lobster claw clasp, and close the jump ring. On the other side, string a 5mm jump ring on the last link of chain. String the doll pendant on the chain.

Materials
- **20** 5-in. (13cm) feathers, fuchsia (craft store)
- 7 ft. (2.1m) 4-ply Irish waxed linen, fuchsia (Royalwood, Ltd.)
- 2 ft. (61cm) 2-ply Irish waxed linen, orange crush (Royalwood, Ltd.)
- 28mm face bead
- 28mm flower wooden bead
- 14mm crocheted circle with beads (M&J Trimming)
- 19mm vintage Japanese flocked plastic spoke bead (Metalliferrous)
- **2** 13mm felted wool balls, red (Tinsel Trading)
- **2** 6mm frosted glass beads, light blue
- 17½ in. (44.5cm) 2mm figaro chain, silver
- 12mm lobster claw clasp with ring, silver
- 5mm 22-gauge jump ring, silver

Tools
- wide-eyed needle (sized to fit through the large figaro chain links)
- diagonal wire cutters or scissors
- **2** pairs of pliers

A Penny for a Buttonhole

Multistrand button necklace

The best gift is a personal gift, and in this case personal meant a box of buttons from a friend of a friend. An afternoon spent color-separating yielded this lovely display of ivory, cream, and off-white (you should see the green pile!). The best part is how the crackled buttons look against gold jewelry wire — a true example of how age and patina accent modern and sheen. I hope my friend of a friend agrees.

Materials

- assortment of similarly hued buttons and rings (about **32**)
- 28 ft. (8.5m) flexible beading wire, .018 or .019, gold
- **2** (20mm) cones, bronze (Ashes to Beauty Adornments)
- hook and clasp, bronze (Ashes to Beauty Adornments)
- **8** 2½ x 3mm mega crimp tubes, gold filled
- 10 in. 20- to 22-gauge wire, gold-filled or German jewelry wire

Tools

- flatnose pliers
- roundnose pliers
- diagonal wire cutters

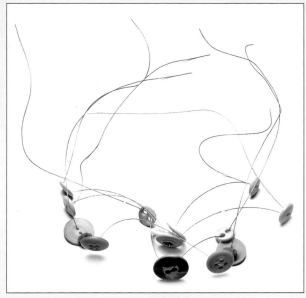

1 Determine the finished length of your necklace (mine is 17 in/43 cm). Cut 16 lengths of beading wire to the following lengths: four that are 2 in. (5cm) longer than your desired length and three additional sets of four, each 2 in. longer than the previous set. Work with one set of four wire strands at a time. Choose a variety of buttons and work the wire through the holes at varying intervals. Be sure to keep all four sets in mind when designing the overall necklace.

DESIGNER'S TIP

Be careful not to use too much pressure to slide the buttons into position; it is easy to end up with curly ribbon wire.

ALTERNATIVE

- Substitute other sewing notions of one type or a mélange of many.
- Use spacers to separate items.

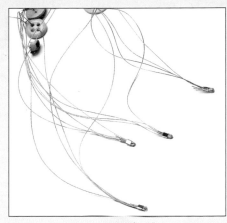

2 Gather the wire ends of each set, string a mega crimp tube, form a loop with the wire ends around the tip of your roundnose pliers, and pass the wire back through the mega crimp tube. Flatten the crimp (see Techniques). Repeat on the other end, and then with each set.

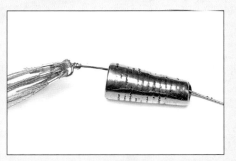

3 Cut a 2-in. length of wire. Make the first half of a wrapped loop at one end, working at the upper third of your roundnose pliers. String the loops of the four wire sets and complete the wraps. Thread the remaining wire end through a cone.

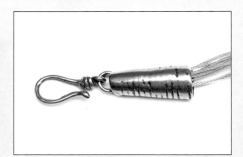

4 Make the first half of a wrapped loop above the cone and string half the clasp. Complete the wraps, and trim the end. Repeat to finish the other side, substituting the other clasp half.

1 Pain... pain...

4 Mea... cord... length m...

5 Add... to th...

The Long Way Around

Tape measure bangle

Ignore the adage to measure twice and cut once. Super easy to put together, you'll be looking for other ways to measure up new jewelry designs. Especially charming for sewing types — that is, if you can part with your wrist pin cushions and tape-measure-as-necklace. Sew very vogue!

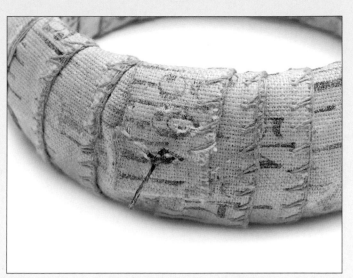

1 Wrap the tape measure around the bangle: Begin with one end of the tape measure at the outside of the bangle and wrap on a diagonal, slightly overlapping each wrap with a new one. Continue until the entire bangle is covered, ending on the outside again (fold the end under, if necessary).

2 Thread the needle with the linen and tack down the tape measure.

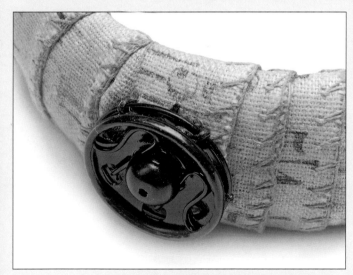

3 Sew the male side of the snap over the stitch, hiding it, and snap on the female side.

4 Sew on the other two snaps at one-third intervals.

Designer's Tip

If you're lucky enough to find a tape measure with metal tab ends, be sure to emphasize these in your design.

Alternative

Sew on one or more vintage buttons instead of coat snaps. Leave the tape measure ends free to set off the buttons.

Materials
- 60 in. (1.5m) cloth tape measure
- ⅝-1-in. (1.6-2.5cm) wide plain wooden bangle
- 24 in. (61cm) Irish waxed linen thread, 2- or 4-ply, black (Royalwood Ltd.)
- 3 large coat snaps or antique buttons

Tools
- wide-eyed needle (curved works best)
- scissors or diagonal wire cutters

Oh! Domin-oh!

Adjustable domino necklace

1 Drill a hole through one end of a domino about ½ in. (1.3cm) from one end.

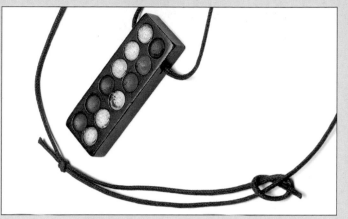

2 Thread the length of waxed cotton cord through the domino, center the pendant and overlap the ends slightly. Tie a square knot (see Techniques) around the length where it ends on one end to form a moving knot. Repeat on the other end.

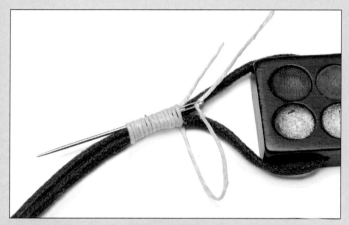

3 Re-center the domino and bring the cords together about 1 in. (2.5cm) above the top of the domino. Wrap the waxed linen thread for about ½ in. (1.3cm) along the doubled cord. Thread the tail under the wraps and trim. (Note: This step is shown with yellow thread for illustration; you'll use linen to match the cord color.)

Materials
- antique domino, any size (mine is 2¾ x 1 in./7 x 2.5cm) (Anima Designs)
- 36 in. (.9m) 2-3mm braided waxed cotton cord (Rings & Things)
- 36 in. 4-ply Irish waxed linen thread, black (Royalwood Ltd.)
- 36 in. 4-ply Irish waxed linen thread, turquoise (Royalwood Ltd.)
- cowry shell

Tools
- Dremel or other hand-held drill with ⅛-in. bit
- scissors or diagonal wire cutters
- wide-eyed needle

4 About ½ in. above the last coil wrap, create another wrap around one cotton strand with the turquoise linen. Tie on a cowry shell at both ends, tracing the runner length up along the back of the shell. Knot the ends and trim the thread, leaving a tail if desired.

ALTERNATIVE

Use other domino types. For plastic versions, be sure to drill through gradually, drilling a little further each time. This keeps the bit from overheating.

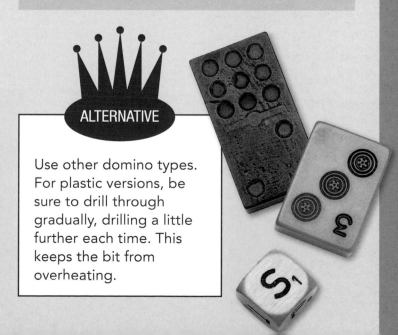

Checkered Past

Checker dangle bangle

After you try this simple resin technique, it will be impossible to play another game with so few checkers left in your set. The lip in this particular checker design just begs to be filled with baubles and resin, and once you get going, it's easy to get carried away. You may miss strategizing your jumps and getting "kinged," but you'll look especially regal wearing this grand bracelet.

ALTERNATIVE

ALTERNATIVE
Try a chess piece or
two – a wrist match!

1 Prepare the checker: Drill a hole in the rim slightly larger than the screw bail. Dot the bail with glue and insert into the hole. Let dry overnight.

2 With the deepest side of the checker facing up, arrange the pearls or beads inside the indentation. Mix the doming resin according to the manufacturer's directions and pour into the checker, filling as much of the indentation as you can. Let dry overnight.

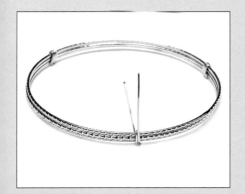

3 Prepare the bangle: Stack thin bracelets sandwiching the gold one between two silver. Cut a 2-in. (5cm) length of wire and make three wraps around the bangles. Trim close and sand smooth. Repeat twice, spacing the wraps about 3 in. (7.6cm) apart.

4 Prepare the dangles: Load the shell pearl onto one ball-tipped head pin and make a wrapped loop (see Techniques) above it. Load the 2mm, 4mm, and 5mm black beads onto another head pin and form a wrapped loop above the top bead.

5 Open the jump ring (Techniques). String the checker component, the pearl charm, the black bead charm, and the bangle. Close the jump ring.

Materials
- 30mm checker with rim
- **13** 3mm pearls or beads
- doming resin (hobby or art supply store)
- screw bail (Rings & Things)
- 14mm shell pearl, ivory
- 5mm round bead, black
- 4mm round bead, matte black
- 2mm round bead, black
- **2** ball-tipped head pins, silver
- **3** thin bangles: two silver, one gold

- 6-8 in. (15-20cm) 22-gauge square wire, sterling silver or gold-filled (optional, round or half-round)
- 8mm jump ring, silver
- E-6000 or Bond 527 glue

Tools
- Dremel or other hand-held drill with ⅟₃₂-in.) bit
- disposable medicine cup and wooden stir stick
- chainnose pliers
- roundnose pliers
- diagonal wire cutters

I Pledge Allegiance ...

Pin-back badge collar

Long before the media defined blue states and red states, politicians campaigned the old-fashioned way — with clever slogans and pin-wearing supporters across the nation. Whatever your current politics, embrace the past and wear your platform front and center.

1 Clean the brass neck piece with alcohol and spray-paint both sides white. (Several light coats followed by drying works best.)

2 Create a paper template by tracing around the collar. Arrange the buttons on the template and mark the top center placement of each badge. Turn each pin so the closed end is placed at the top, center.

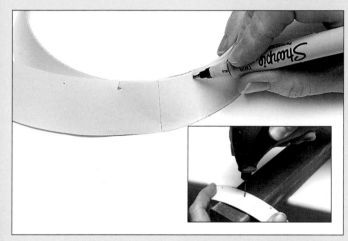

3 Transfer the marks to the collar with an extra-fine-tip marker. Drill the holes.

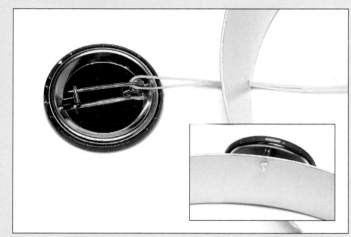

4 Cut 6 in. (15cm) of linen for each button and fold in half. Wrap the folded linen around the closed end of the pin and thread both ends through the hole in the collar, front to back. Knot with a surgeon's knot, trim, and dot carefully with glue.

Materials
- collection of small pins (Julee Zawalick)
- 1 or 1¼-in. (2.5-3.2cm) brass collar (Designer Findings)
- 4-6 ft. (1.2-1.8m) 4-ply Irish waxed linen thread, any color (Royalwood, Ltd.)
- G-S Hypo Cement or cyanoacrylate glue
- alcohol
- white spray paint, satin finish or spray lacquer

Tools
- extra-fine-tip permanent marker
- scissors
- chainnose pliers
- low-profile topless box to spray paint
- Dremel or other hand-held drill with small bit

Alternatives
Make your own badges with a button maker and pictures cut from your favorite magazines.

If you like the brass look, just clean with alcohol and spray the neck piece with lacquer to set the finish and prevent it from aging.

Pin-up

Laundry pin bohemian necklace

This brass pin was used in the army as a laundry help, to keep bags securely together and to identify the owner. Now paired with a medley of metals and miscellany, the necklace becomes a modern set of dog tags pinning you as trend-ready.

1 Create charm components: a) attach a 5mm gold-filled jump ring (see Techniques) to the bronze bird charm, a 5mm silver jump ring to the mum charm, and 8mm jump rings to the brass African fetish ring and the carved wood donut; b) load the three freshwater pearls onto one ball-tipped head pin and the vintage yellow bead to another, and create a wrapped loop (Techniques) on each just above the topmost bead; c) use the wire to attach a wrapped loop with swing (Techniques) to the turquoise carved leaf.

2 Add the yellow bead, carved leaf, and bird charm components to a 6mm gold-filled jump ring.

3 Open an 8mm gold-filled jump ring and string the tri-charm component, the end links from the gunmetal curb chain, the gold-filled figure 8 chain, and the vintage army laundry pin loop. Close the jump ring.

4 Measure up the gunmetal chain 9 in. (23cm) and the gold-filled chain 12 in. (30cm). Attach a 5mm jump ring at this point, adding in the silver figaro chain 4½ in. (11.4cm) from one end.

5 Open an 8mm jump ring, and string the Hill Tribes silver ring charm, the jump ring of the African ring, and a link of gold and gunmetal chain 3½ in. (8.9cm) from the pin loop. (Note: A swag of gold chain now forms from above.)

6 Add the freshwater pearl component to another 8mm jump ring. Then, gather and add the end links of the figaro (the longest length), the figure 8, and the gunmetal curb chain. Close the jump ring. (Note: The short figaro length remains left out.)

7 Attach the wooden donut charm to the figure 8 chain at the same point where the silver figaro chain tendril ends.

8 Attach the vintage mum component to the end of the remaining figaro chain length.

Materials

- vintage brass army laundry pin
- 13mm bronze bird charm (Ashes to Beauty Adornments)
- 12mm brass African trade bead ring
- 26mm carved wood donut
- 11mm brass and plastic mum charm
- 33 x 14mm carved yellow turquoise leaf pendant
- 12mm vintage yellow glass bead
- 19mm Hill Tribes silver ring charm (Kamol)
- 3 7mm freshwater pearls
- 14 in. (36cm) 2mm silver figaro chain
- 22 in. (56cm) 3mm matte gold-filled figure 8 chain
- 19 in. (48cm) 3mm gunmetal curb chain
- 8mm jump ring, gold-filled
- 2 5mm jump rings, gold-filled
- 4 8mm jump rings, sterling silver
- 2 5mm jump rings, sterling silver
- 2 2-in. (5cm) ball-tipped head pins, brass or gold-filled
- 6 in. (15cm) 22-gauge sterling silver or silver German jewelry wire

Tools

- roundnose pliers
- chainnose pliers
- diagonal wire cutters

DESIGNER'S TIP

The brass mum charm that adorns the loose tendril can continue around the neck or drop seductively down the back.

Camo-Bling

Army belt cuff

The easiest way to take inches off your waist: Simply shorten an old camouflage belt to wrist length and embellish. Bling's the thing that jazzes up this army drab, but don't count on blending in anymore – you'll stand out at roll call and beyond.

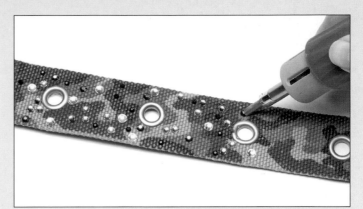

1 Try the belt on your wrist, noting where you should cut the end and where to avoid placing crystals. Remove either the buckle or the metal tip. Cut the belt and reattach the buckle or tip to the raw end.

2 Arrange the crystals in a pleasing manner directly on the belt. (Note: Avoid placing flat-back crystals under the area where the buckle closes.) Carefully adhere the crystals with the applicator using the appropriate tip for each size. (I started with the size for which I had the largest quantity, thus decreasing my chances of bumping and moving my design.)

3 Cut and sand the screw off the back of the army pins with a cutting bit, then a sanding bit.

4 Glue the pin back to the backing and the whole pin component to the top of the buckle.

designer's tip
If your crystals are not adhering, chances are you are using the wrong tip. Try another, or substitute G-S Hypo Cement.

alternative
Fill the buckle top with other military designations, i.e., bars, pins, etc.

Materials
- old army web belt with slide buckle
- **20-30** 3-4mm Swarovski flat-back hot-fix crystals (I used jonquil, light Colorado topaz, topaz, light smoke topaz, blue zircon, jet)
- antique army pins
- E-6000, Bond 527, or G-S Hypo Cement

Tools
- scissors
- flatnose or chainnose pliers
- hot-fix crystal applicator with a variety of tips
- Dremel or other hand-held drill with cutting and sanding bits

Yooper Birthstone

Copper ore nugget pendant and necklace

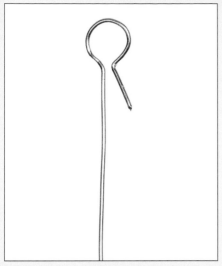

1 Make a wonky wrap to capture the nugget by beginning a wrapped loop (see Techniques) at one end of a length of copper wire, but stop short of wrapping the tail. You should have a 5mm open circle with a ¼-in. (6mm) extension at the end. Shape the tail as pictured.

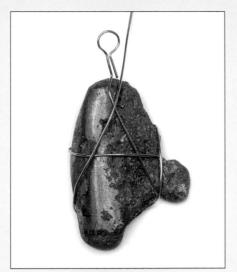

2 Place the open circle with the extension atop the copper ore nugget as shown. Begin to wrap all around the nugget. Finish the wrap coming from the opposite side as you started, so that the nugget is encased within the wire cage. End at the bottom of the loop.

3 Wrap haphazardly around the loop, filling in the area between the nugget and the open loop. Trim the excess wire. Set the pendant aside.

4 Cut six 1-in. (2.5cm) pieces of 22-gauge copper wire. Create eye pins by forming a plain loop (Techniques) at one end of each piece. Be sure to make the eyes big enough to prevent them from going through a chain link. Lay the copper chain lengths parallel and designate six points at which to add the eye-pin components. Insert an eye pin through the outside chain at the first point, load a turquoise rondelle, go through the inside chain at the first point, and create another plain loop to complete the connection. Repeat at the other five points.

5 Open a 4mm jump ring (Techniques). String the end links of both chains and half the clasp. Close the jump ring. Repeat on the other end.

Materials
- copper ore nugget
- 28 in. (71cm) oval chain, copper
- 28 in. figaro chain, copper
- 6 4mm rondelles, rough turquoise
- 3 ft. (.9m) 22-gauge wire, copper
- 2 4mm jump rings
- 2 6mm jump rings
- 7mm snap clasp, copper

Tools
- chainnose pliers
- roundnose pliers
- diagonal wire cutters

6 Open two 6mm jump rings. String the pendant through its loop onto both rings. Close the rings around the center of the two chains, so the pendant can slide at the bottom of the necklace.

Alternative
This wrapping technique is useful for any type of undrilled treasure. Use it for other gemstones and rocks, sea glass, acorns, marbles, etc.

Rock Locket

Split stone locket and
netted amulet

It's serendipitous when you cull a perfectly split stone from a patch of gravel. The same stone turns sentimental when fashioned into a locket. And, a favorite photo of my Gram, an "M" for her name, Mae, and a feather for her love of nature, completes the picture.

1 Make the locket: Tear a resized photo from its background. Arrange the photo, feather piece, and initial in a mini-collage. (Note: Flat pieces were used here so that the rock would still fit together.) Adhere the items to the face of the back stone with gel medium. Let dry overnight.

2 Net the locket: Cut three 1 yd. (.9m) pieces of linen. Align them and at the center, take one of the strands from the right side and form four coil wraps around the other two. Anchor the coil at the other end with a square knot (see Techniques). (This forms the bottom of the amulet net.)

3 With the two top center strands, tie a square knot (Techniques) about ¼-in. (6mm) above the coil wrap. Split the ties from this knot and form two more square knots flanking this one.

4 Add in the rock, face side up, placing the initial coil wrap at the bottom center. Working close to the rock, tie square knots up the sides and front (keep fairly low here to accommodate the embellishment while catching in both rock pieces).

5 Work square knots up the back, finally tying in the side knots. End with two knots at the top of each side.

6 Tie a slip knot (Techniques) on the front of the rock at top center. Trim the ends 3-5 in. (7.6-13cm) from the slip knot. (Note: Finish ends by trimming on the diagonal and rolling the tips between your fingers.)

7 Center the washer on the rock within the net opening, and glue.

8 Make the strap: Cut two 1-yd. pieces of linen. Align the linen and make overhand knots every 3-4 in. (7.6-10cm). Add a gunmetal jump ring to the amulet netting just below the final overhand knot. Tie the strap onto the ring with a square knot, leaving a 2-3 in. (5-7.6cm) tail. Repeat on the other side.

9 With a 6-in. (15cm) length of linen, tie on the whole feather.

Materials
- split stone (or other two-part item)
- photo, reduced to fit
- Mod Podge or other gel medium, matte
- internal tooth washer, or other small metal embellishment
- feather and feather piece
- initial torn from an old missalette page
- 6 yd. (5.5m) 4-ply Irish waxed linen thread, black
- E-6000 or Bond 527
- 2 6mm gunmetal jump rings

Tools
- small brush
- scissors
- 2 pairs of pliers

DESIGNER'S TIP
- If digital resizing with a computer and or scanner is not an option, visit your local copy shop and use a copy machine to resize your photo.

ALTERNATIVE
- Use an old hinge as an alternate locket form and hang it from chain.
- Add photos to both sides.

A Joy to Have in Class

Gold star sticker
cascading earrings

Getting a gold star on your home-work certainly boosted your confidence as a kid. Now, combining the stars and colored pailettes gets you self-approval any time you need an extra lift. Especially useful during moments of self doubt, these ear-rings tell the world you're the best.

1 Cut the figaro chain into 10 lengths of 2 in. (5cm) each (set aside one set of five lengths). Attach a chain to each of the five loops of the earring tops with 5mm jump rings (see Techniques).

Materials
- 8 20mm pailettes, 4 blue and 4 clear (M&J Trimming)
- star stickers: 8 gold and 8 silver (teaching stores such as The Learning Shop)
- 45 in. (1.1m) 3mm figaro chain, silver
- 8 star charms: 2 16mm gold, 2 16mm silver, 2 13mm gold, 2 10mm silver
- 2 5-hole earring tops or connector bars, silver
- 18 5mm jump rings, silver
- 8 7mm jump rings, silver
- pair of earring wires

Tools
- 2 pairs of pliers
- diagonal wire cutters

Alternative
Pailettes look even more fabulous in layers. Create a similar earring with 5 strands of shimmering layered pailettes. Alternate bold colors or create a monochromatic version to match your next evening gown.

2 Add gold and silver star stickers to the front and back of four blue pailettes and four clear pailettes. (Note: On the clear pailettes, align the back stars carefully to match the front stars.)

3 Add the pailettes with 7mm jump rings and the star charms with 5mm jump rings to the chain segments as desired, placing one star charm on the earring top's upper loop.

4 Open the loop of an earring wire and attach the loop of the earring top (Techniques). Make a second earring to match the first.

Necklace in a Flash

Flashcard layered necklace

School-day memories surface easily when they are this close to heart. The combination of a beautiful Japanese fiber in two vibrant colors, a mitten clip, and a well-chosen flashcard can take you back to those snowy mornings when you sat next to the radio, fingers crossed, wishing for a snow day.

21

mittens

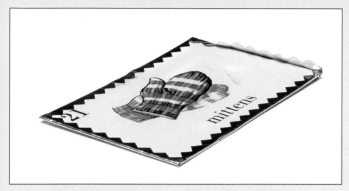

1 Measure, cut, and adhere silver foil tape to the edges of a flashcard, overlapping the corners for a smooth finish. (I trimmed the foil tape with pinking shears for a decorative edge.)

Materials

- 36 in. (.9m) blue yarn (Habu Textiles)
- 36 in. orange yarn (Habu Textiles)
- mitten clip (sewing store)
- 34 in. (86cm) 7 x 9mm heavy hammered curb chain, silver (Rings & Things)
- 3 in. x 1¾ in. (7.6cm x 4.4cm) vintage flashcard
- 1 ft. (30cm) ¼-in. (6mm) silver foil tape (stamping or paper crafts store)
- 4 8mm jump rings, silver
- foldover clasp, silver (Rings & Things)
- fabric glue

Tools

- scissors
- bone folder or burnishing tool (optional)
- diagonal wire cutters
- wide-eyed needle

2 Cut two 7½-in. (19.1cm) lengths of chain and one 18-in. (46cm) length. Add the two shorter lengths to either side of the mitten clip with 8mm jump rings (see Techniques).

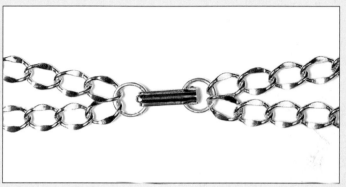

3 Open an 8mm jump ring, and string the remaining end of the 7½-in. chain, one end of the 18-in. chain, and one clasp channel. Close the jump ring. Repeat on the other side.

4 Thread a wide-eyed needle with both yarn lengths. Weave the yarn back and forth through each link of the 18-in. chain. (Note: Chain length will decrease by several inches with this step.)

5 Come around the last link and thread back through the chain and yarn. End in a thin place, hiding the end. Trim close, and dot with fabric glue. Repeat on the other end. Attach the flashcard to the mitten clip.

ALTERNATIVE

For a fun, yet practical solution to the I.D. tag dilemma, clip on your school or hospital I.D. instead of a kitschy flashcard.

Sharpener Image

Sharpened pencil brooch

When a certain young man visits the pencil sharpener a little too often, trade him your new No. 2 for the stubby nubs he's left behind. Using coiling (a basket weaving technique) and just the right size spring to adorn the miserly leftovers, you'll get a colorful and useful pin out of the deal.

1 If you are not already working with old pencils, prepare new ones by breaking them in half (score around the diameter of the pencil, then break at the score mark). Sharpen the end you would like for your pin. Cut springs in varying sizes with toolbox cutters and add a few to each pencil.

2 Arrange the pencils and mark and drill holes that will connect the pencil set at about ⅜ in. (1cm) from the tips.

3 Cut the length of linen in half. Tie a knot at the end of one piece of linen, leaving a 2-in. (5cm) tail. Thread through the pencils, securing with a knot tight to the other side.

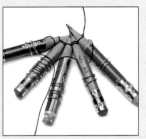

4 Begin to coil the linen around the first pencil, then up and down through the pencil set, pulling the linen tight against the pencils and each other. Proceed back and forth, looping around each end and back again. At the ¼-in. (6mm) point, ending at the opposite side of the first knot, add the second linen length with a knot (this acts as an anchor point for the pin back).

5 Continue the pattern for about ½ in. (1.3cm), ending at the site of the first knot.

6 Knot. Dot the pin back with a few drops of glue and tie it on with the tail ends.

designer's tips
- If your pencils are a tad big for the springs, they chew up the paint, leaving a wonderful chipped finish on the ridges.
- If you don't have a spring, wrap German jewelry wire around the pencils, and trim.

alternative
To convert this pin into a pendant, add a bail instead of a pin back.

Materials
- **5** or **6** pencils
- **5** or **6** springs to fit pencils
- 4-6 yards (3.7-5.5m) 2-ply Irish waxed linen thread, black
- 1 in. (2.5cm) pin back
- G-S Hypo Cement

Tools
- toolbox cutters
- scissors
- pencil sharpener
- Dremel or other hand-held drill with ⅟₃₂-in. bit

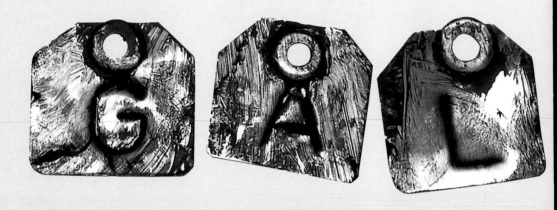

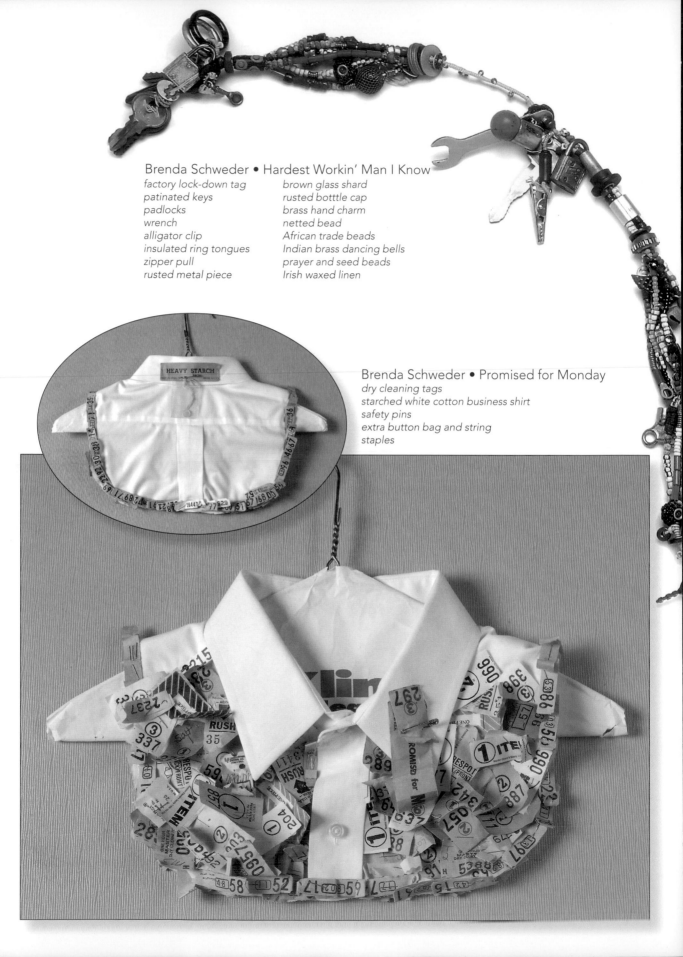

Brenda Schweder • Hardest Workin' Man I Know

factory lock-down tag
patinated keys
padlocks
wrench
alligator clip
insulated ring tongues
zipper pull
rusted metal piece

brown glass shard
rusted botttle cap
brass hand charm
netted bead
African trade beads
Indian brass dancing bells
prayer and seed beads
Irish waxed linen

Brenda Schweder • Promised for Monday

dry cleaning tags
starched white cotton business shirt
safety pins
extra button bag and string
staples

Brenda Schweder • One Woman's Junque

doorbell escutcheon
brass cloak clip
Afghani signature stamp
garter belt component
celluloid "pull"
reclaimed hammered
  pendant with light-pull
  chain
cabochon with hand-
  knotted net
bone donut with mesh
  ribbon

wire-wrapped slate
Hindu Ganesha pendant
brass hand pendant
assorted Hill Tribes silver
  charms and beads
assorted buttons
glass rings
sterling silver and nickel
  chain
Irish waxed linen

Brenda Schweder •
Clip & Clasp Reincarnate
rhinestone dress clip/clasp
stamped metal flower
cicada beads
reclaimed faux pearl
sterling silver chain
pewter clasp

Brenda Schweder • Diva Leopardess or
Camouflage Enhanced Is Camouflage No More
plastic toy leopard
Swarovski flat-backed crystals
steel cable and magnetic clasp

Brenda Schweder •
Sugar-coated
Cute 'n Cuddly
lamb appliqué
seed bead wired flower
crocheted daffodil
yarn pom-pom
Irish waxed linen
sterling silver clasp
vintage glass beads
vintage glass ring
rose and pineapple quartz
Mokuba velvet ribbon

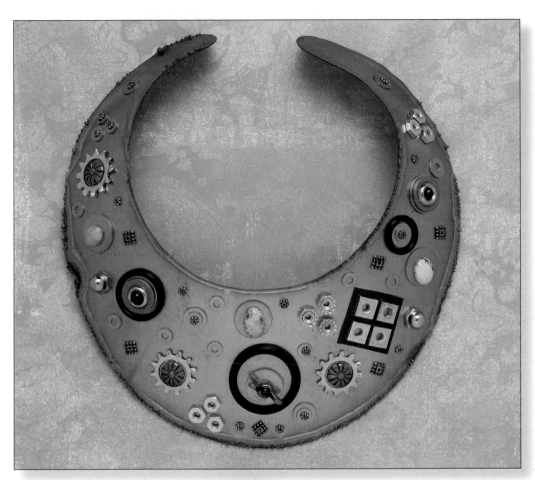

Rebecca Conrad-LaMere • Ace Hardware 101
sheet copper
bronze thrust bearings
thumb tacks
O rings
wing, hex, acorn,
  square, and spinning
  lock nuts
toothed lock, finishing,
  and copper washers
copper beads
garnet
star sapphire
turquoise

Becki Moylan • Seeking Balance
metal button
beach stone
handpainted tree
resistors
circuitry
sea blue chalcedony

Susan Lenart Kazmer • Talisman
sterling
brass
silk
found objects

Photo by Denise Andersen,
daphotoart.com

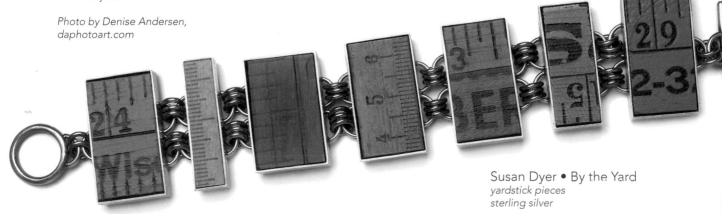

Susan Dyer • By the Yard
yardstick pieces
sterling silver

Carla Sikorski • Tea Time
tea ball
seed beads
metal beads
charm
chain

Helen Dahms •
Chain Smoker
cigar tips
resin-coated cigar labels
seed beads
Swarovski crystals
extension springs
brass chain
brass clasp

Diane Marshall

Women's Work
fabricated copper
antique photo
sewing notions

My Life Is Going Up In Flames
matches
fabricated nickel

Keith Lo Bue •
An Absent Man
Art deco ladies'
compact case
etched and oxidized
copper and brass
steel animal trap jaw
silver fork
keys
coin
drawer hardware
ivory fan
optometrist test
lenses
glass bead
eucalyptus seeds
opal
19th-century litho-
graph and engraving
watch gear and
winding crown
leather
paper
text
soil

Photo by Keith Lo Bue

Ann Cook • With Time
brass watch parts
brass chain
bead

Bonnie DeSautelle •
Caffeine and Crystals
beach glass
Swarovski crystal
seed beads
chain

Pam Kehoe-Peterson •
A Question of Balance
sterling silver
steel
brass
copper
key and caliper parts
bubble level
hand-stamped text

Photo by Larry Sanders

Resources

American Science & Surplus
847-647-0011
sciplus.com
You know you've joined the World of Geekdom when you shop this store more than once. It's a good thing (much different than Martha's Good Thing), though, 'cause all the weird and wacky widgets and wonders that sit on the shelves exercise your brain with idea after madcap idea.

Anima Designs
412-726-8401
animadesigns.com
The collage artist's heaven. Peruse this site for oddities and other goofy, but necessary stuff — like milagros or vintage dominos or Mexican playing cards or . . . (Just watch your time while surfing this site — obsessive behavior is only a few clicks away.)

Ashes to Beauty Adornments
505-899-8864
ashes2beauty.com
Sweet Rene! She and husband, Len, schlep reproduction ethnographic beads and charms around the country for us. If their product doesn't win you over, Rene will. She emanates sunshine (well, sunshine with a little funnel-cloud action). Check out her site for the embellishments line (GREAT for doll-makers and doodad lovers alike).

Designer's Findings
262-574-1324
designersfindings.net
The lovely and talented Diane Hyde owns this hard-to-find and unusual findings company. When I want 'inventive' to do 'innovative,' I call Diane. LOVE the mesh products, and the pin-back brooches got me the cover of *BeadStyle*, so what can I say?

Eclectica
262-641-0910
eclecticabeads.com
My local haunt — it's where I go for just about everything from beads to findings to tools. In TV terms, it's my Cheers, 'cept I don't have my own bar stool yet.

Green Girl
828-298-2263
greengirlstudios.com
During my very first *Bead&Button* Show, I blew the majority of my checking account (they're in the first row) and my allotted time (three hours — what can I say, I was a bead virgin) here. Wee (as Cynthia puts it) Artistry (as I dub it) — Green Girl puts whimsy in the bead world.

Habu Textiles
212-239-3546
habutextiles.com
Wow! An NYC retail showroom chock-a-block full of unique fibers and yarns from wool and cotton to bamboo and paper. If you visit and you're a fiber-holic, leave two hours minimum just to make up your mind!

Julee Zawalick
wisconsinantiquedealers.com
Julee's really knowledgeable about wee things in the antique world. Her little animal figurines are to die for and the variety she carries is mind-blowing.

Kamol Beads
206-764-7375
My friends, Kamol and Becky (at least they treat me like a dear friend) sell the BEST Thai Hill Tribes silver and Nepalese beads, pendants, and lovelies. My beading buddies know better than to wait for me when I stop at their booth — it's not a PDQ experience, that's for sure!

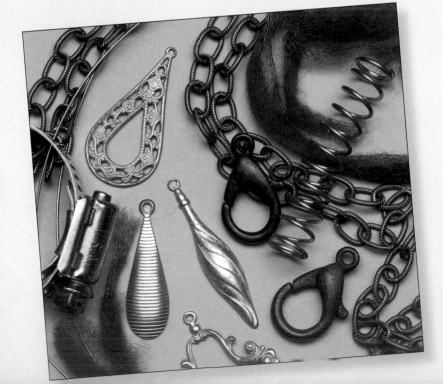

Metalliferous
888-944-0909
metalliferous.com
Second floor, please. Worth finding, this New York cubbyhole (not small, but packed) of a store is separated down the middle. I culled through the entire bead side (left leg, in pants terms) and rewarded myself with some kitschy Japanese vintage paper and plain ol' injection-molded plastic beads. Splendiferous!

M&J Trimming
800-965-8746
mjtrim.com/index.aspx
This place astounded me. Only in New York would mini-shopping carts be in a trim store. Floor to ceiling schtuff in little boxes. Can't wait to visit again.

Ornamentea
919-834-6260
ornamentea.com
Super-duper findings in super-duper finishes. If I lived closer, you might need the number to find me. But it's a plane ride away, so I take advantage of the EXCELLENT customer service (phone or Web).

Rings & Things
800-366-2156
rings-things.com
Because this is one of the first places I bought wholesale, I have a special place in my heart for it. R&T has a great variety of shapes and cuts of semiprecious stones AND staff members who travel the country to sell direct so they continue to drive up my Visa bill!

Rio Grande
800-545-6566
riogrande.com
The jewelry maker's staple. This is where I look to find the new stuff I HAVE to have. Sometimes I just sit and page through their new catalog when it comes for inspiration. Gee . . . .

Royalwood Ltd.
800-526-1630
royalwoodltd.com
The only place I know that sells such a great color array of Irish waxed linen. And, if you use 4-ply (which will work for most anything I do), you can choose from a virtual rainbow. I never knew I'd have such an ample personal collection. I LOVE this stuff!

Stone Mountain Colorado
719-738-3991
Ya' gotta' love Stone Mountain for the unusual. I got the brass charms for the drawer pull bracelet and the little yellow glass flowers for the bumble bee ring here. ALL your goodies are weighed at checkout — now, that's an experience!

Tinsel Trading Company
212-730-1030
tinseltrading.com
My very FAVE New York haunt. I just know Sarah Jessica shops here when she's looking for favors for that special reunion dinner for the S&TC cast. Wonderful trim, appliqué, et al. I even found the silliest reproduction bobby pins there.

Toho Shoji
212-868-7465
tohoshojiny.com
When in New York (or Japan, I suppose) you need to visit! They carry some unique findings and even neater gotta-have's.

Vintaj Natural Brass Co.
vintaj.com
If you like brass like I do, Vintaj will stir your heart. The coolest things are the filigree stampings that you can wrap as a bezel — I had never thought of that!

Acknowledgments

Many heartfelt thanks and a boatload of love to:

My gallery artists

For your brilliant contributions to making this book all I wanted it to be and for your inspiration to me and the readers of this book.

My many Kalmbachian cohorts

- Pat Lantier; without her support and ability to find the glimmer in me, this book would have not been possible.

- Karin Buckingham and Lisa Bergman, who extended my vision and made it a visual reality beyond my expectations.

- Jim Forbes and Bill Zuback, whose photo-artistry leaves me in awe.

- Mark Thompson, Lesley Weiss, Salena Safranski, and all in Books.

- Mindy Brooks, who gave me my true start in published jewelry, and Sandra Keiser, my college professor and now Fashion Forecast writing partner and friend.

- Naomi Fujimoto and Cathy Jakicic, my *BeadStyle* editors, who keep asking for more.

- Linda Augsburg and all the jewelry-title ladies.

- Debbi Simon, my co-con-inspirer.

- Marlene Vail, Linda Kollatz, Joel Wingelman, the B&B Show team, and all who have assisted me in the trade-show realm.

- Laurie Stafforini and all the other smiling Kalmbachians who continually greet me and help carry my toppling towers through the halls when I visit (yes, you, Mike!).

My top cheerleaders

- Mom and Dad, who when it comes right down to the important stuff of life, deny me nothing.

- My brothers and sisters, especially Joanne, and their wonderful mates and kiddos.

- Luci Link; together we're one hell-of-a-woman.

- Lela Joscelyn, my longtime back-patter and galpal.

- Dawn Oertel, the softer, stitchier side of craft.

- Beth Shaw, who encourages me by chiding that I'll never make my deadlines, and Chloe Drapes, her daughter, whose love I can only hope to repay in full.

- Taisha Weber, chief cheerleader, yogi-style.

- Julia Miller, my words revised.

- Ann Cook, my friend. Dear, sweet, and true.

- Helen Dahms, the living angel on my shoulder.

- Carla Sikorski, my right-hand "woman."

- All the other A.T. Gals and the W.E. Women, remarkable as they all are!

My angels

- Sister Remy Revor. The *Velveteen Rabbit* devotee, she took me aside and told me, "I believe you can do whatever you put your mind to." You will remain my REAL mentor forever.

- John and Mae Chelmecki, my grandparents, who proclaimed me an artist and made my childhood "the whole box of 64 Crayolas."

- Uncle Bobby Schweder, whose tough tree wrangler's body radiated a boyish playfulness beyond compare.

My shining stars

My sons, Jimmy and Liam, who keep me (somewhat) tethered and allow me to pilfer their toys in the name of art.

My one and only

My Mr. Black-and-White (I'm his every-colored wife) husband, Jim. After 14 years, he's softened a bit to my curiosities. In the middle of mowing the lawn one day, he approached me sheepishly (he's still not quite sure of the whys to this mild obsession), extending a tiny budded branch. He muttered, "Thought you may want to have this" and went back to work. I teared up. It was my bouquet of perfect roses, my box of Godiva chocolates, my sweet Valentine. Funny what a little found object can bring!

About the Author

Brenda Schweder is a self-professed *Junque-ess*. Collector of all things intriguing, her creative career started in silkscreen, collage, and assemblage and her work was shown in galleries and art shows. A segue into the world of jewelry design was spawned when she accepted the gig to co-author *BeadStyle's* Fashion Forecast. Brenda is now a frequent contributor to *BeadStyle* and has been published in *Art Jewelry* and *Bead&Button* magazines, as well as a number of other pamphlets and books. Her business, Brenda Schweder Jewelry, offers fashion-forward jewelry via her Web site, www.brendaschweder.com.

Brenda lives in Waukesha, Wisconsin, with her found husband and not-at-all altered sons.